EASTERN ARABIC-ENGLISH
ENGLISH-EASTERN ARABIC
DICTIONARY AND PHRASEBOOK

EASTERN ARABIC-ENGLISH
ENGLISH-EASTERN ARABIC
DICTIONARY AND PHRASEBOOK

for the Spoken Arabic of Jordan, Lebanon,
Palestine/Israel and Syria

HIPPOCRENE BOOKS
New York

Copyright © 1998 Hippocrene Books, Inc.
Second printing, 2002.

ISBN 0-7818-0685-2

For information, address:
HIPPOCRENE BOOKS, INC.
171 Madison Avenue
New York, NY 10016

Printed in the United States of America.

CONTENTS

INTRODUCTION

The Arabic language is spoken today throughout an area that lies partly in Asia and partly in Africa. The eastern part of this region is the Zagros Mountains, dividing Iraq from Iran; the western boundary is the Atlantic Ocean off the coast of Morocco. In the north the boundary is the Taurus range, dividing Turkey from Syria and Iraq, and in the South the Indian Ocean, the eastern and central regions of Africa, and the Sahara Desert.

Though Arabic is the everyday speech of most of the inhabitants of the region described above, it would be a mistake to assume that they all speak the same kind of Arabic. Arabic has shared the fate of all languages that are spread over a large area for a long period of time. It has developed a wide variety of dialects, some of them being so different from one another that they might almost be considered separate languages. The mutual understanding of different dialects depends, as in the case of other languages, upon the dialects themselves and upon the educational background and cultural bias of the speakers.

Apart from spoken Arabic, with its many dialects, there is the literary language, frequently called Classical Arabic. This is basically the language of the Koran and early literature. Classical Arabic is the accepted standard for all written material, but it is not used as a language of everyday conversation. As a spoken language it is confined to certain socially prescribed occasions, such as on the radio and in public addresses. It is necessary to understand that no Arab grows up speaking classical Arabic. Each Arab grows up speaking a modern dialect and learns the classical at school.

The spoken Arabic of the Levant, historically denominating Jordan, Lebanon, Syria, and Palestine, is as rich in vocabulary and expressions and as diversified in pronunciation as are the dialects in all other parts of the Arab world. But the colloquial of the Levant has many similarities too, which defines it as Eastern Arabic and present it as the spoken language widely understood in all countries of the region.

Featuring an intentionally easy-to-use pronunciation system in English, this book is designed for anyone who wishes to familiarize themselves with the spoken Arabic of the Levant or plans a trip to the region. It provides the traveler with basic key vocabulary and useful phrases for day-to-day life.

PRONUNCIATION GUIDE

The variety of Arabic presented and described in this book has twenty-seven consonants and five vowels, indicated by letter symbols. Both consonants and vowels occur short (indicated by a single symbol: r, a) and long (indicated by doubling the symbol: rr, aa). The distinction between short and long is very important, as it may distinguish otherwise identical words: mara *woman* beside marra *once*, safar *travel* beside saafar *he traveled*.

THE CONSONANTS

Plain: b d f g G h H j k l m q r s š t w x y z ' "

Velarized: **D S T Z**

Most of the **plain consonants** have near equivalents in English or some of the more familiar languages of Europe.

b	like *b* in *bit*: baab *door*
d	like *d* in *dip*: dawa *medicine*
f	like *f* in *fit*: fihim *he understood*
g	like *g* in *get*: siigaara *cigarette*
G	like the *r* in Parisian French *mari*: Gaali *expensive*
h	like the *h* in *hot*: haada *this*
j	like the *s* in *measure*: jaab *he brought*
k	like *k* in *kit*: katab *he wrote*
l	like the *l* in German *Lied*; a "clear" l, not like the l in *deal*: laazim *necessary*
m	like the *m* in *met*: maktab *office*
n	like the *n* in *net*: naas *people*
r	like the *r* in Spanish *pero* when short: mara *woman*, like the *rr* in Spanish *perro* when long: marra *once*

s	like the *s* in *sit*: saadis *sixth*
š	like the *sh* in *ship*: šaaf *he saw*
t	like the *t* in *tip*: taamin *eighth*
w	like the *w* in *wet*: walad *child*
x	like the *ch* in German *ach*: xaamis *fifth*
y	like the *y* in *yet*: yoom *day*
z	like the *z* in *zinc*: zeet *oil*

The following plain consonants have no equivalents as distinctive sounds in English or the more familiar languages of Europe:

'	a quick çatch in the throat before, between, or after vowels: 'aal *he said*, sa'al *he asked*, suu' *market*; this sound is called "glottal stop".
q	a *k*-sound made at a point somewhat behind the *c* in English *cool*: qisim *part*, maqaale *article*
H	a hissing *h*-sound made by lowering the back of the tongue and and tightening the muscles of the throat: Habb *he liked*, waaHad *one*, raaH *he went*
"	a somewhat strained vowel-like sound, produced like H above, but with the vocal cords vibrating: "arabi *Arabic*, na"am *yes*, baa" *he sold*

The **velarized consonants** (also called "emphatic" or "heavy" consonants) are basically like their plain counterparts, but have an accompanying secondary articulation: the back of the tongue is raised toward the soft palate, and the whole tongue is slightly retraced. This secondary articulation modifies the contact surfaces of the tongue in producing the consonants and alters the shape of the mouth cavity in producing the neighboring vowels. The effect on the vowels is the most striking acoustically.

The following list shows words with plain consonants paired with otherwise identical words containing velarized consonants.

Plain			Velarized		
t	**taab**	he repented	T	**Taab**	he recovered
	batt	he decided	T	**baTT**	ducks
d	**faadi**	savior	D	**faaDi**	empty
s	**saaHib**	pulling	S	**SaaHib**	friend
z	**zaahir**	shining	Z	**Zaahir**	appearing

THE VOWELS

long: **ii uu ee oo aa**

short: **i u e o a**

Most of the vowels have close equivalents in English, but the following descriptions are only approximate:

ii	like the *ea* in *beat*: jiib *bring!*
uu	like the *oo* in *boot*: šuuf *look*
ee	like the *ai* in *bait*: beet *house*
oo	like the *oa* in *boat*: yoom *day*
aa	like the *a* in *hat*: kaan *he was*

In the neighborhood of velarized consonants these vowels are considerably modified by the secondary articulation of tongue-raising and retraction: *ii* and *ee* are centered, *uu* and *oo* are retracted, *aa* resembles the *a* in *father*, with retraction.

The short vowels show more variation than the long ones.

i	at the end of a word, like Arabic *ii* above but shorter; in the middle of a word, like the *i* in *bit*: nisi *he forgot*
u	at the end of a word, like Arabic *uu* above but shorter; in the middle of a word, like the *u* in *put*: kuntu *you (pl) were*
e	like Arabic *ee* above but shorter: sitte *six*. In the middle of a word, this sound only occurs in borrowings.

| o | like Arabic *oo* above but shorter: jibto *I brought it*. In the middle of a word, this sound only occurs in borrowings. |
| a | at the end of a word, between the *a* in *father* and the *u* in *but*; in the middle of a word, varying between the *e* in *get* and the *a* in *cut*, depending on the neighboring consonant: bada *he began*, Haka *he spoke* |

In the neighborhood of velarized consonants, *i* and *u* resemble the *e* in *wanted* (as pronounced by most speakers of English), with the lips rounded for *u*; *a* is between the *a* in *father* and the *u* in *but*, with retraction; *o* is lowered; *e* does not occur.

WORD STRESS

Every Arabic word of more than one syllable has one prominent syllable that stands out above the others when the word is pronounced in isolation. This prominence is called stress, and in the following examples will indicate its position by an accent mark (´) over the vowel of the prominent syllable.

For the great majority of words the place of the stress is automatically determined by definite rules. If the word contains a "long" syllable (defined as a syllable that contains either a long vowel or a short vowel followed by two or more consonants), the stress falls on the long syllable that stands nearest the end of the word: Háalak *your condition*; mabSúuT *well*; mabSuuTíin *well* (pl); tfáDDal *please*; šukrán *thanks*. Otherwise the stress falls on the first syllable: 'ána *I*.

Since the position of the stress is almost completely automatic, we shall mark it in this books only for words that do not conform to the rules stated above.

A VERY BASIC GRAMMAR

The following notes explain certain points arising from the phrases, while other grammatical points are dealt with as they arise in the text.

NOUNS

Nouns in Arabic show two grammatical genders, traditionally labeled masculine and feminine.

The typical marker of the feminine noun is the ending -e/-a. The choice of -e or -a is almost completely determined by the nature of the consonant that immediately precedes the ending. If it is a throat consonant (x G q h " H ') or a velarized consonant (T D S Z) the ending is -a. After r it is usually -a, occasionally -e. After all the other consonants it is -e. There are a few exceptions. Now here are a few feminine words:

'uuDa	room
jarriide	newspaper
Taawle	table

ARTICLES

There is no indefinite article in Arabic. The noun stands alone. For example:

finjaan	means *cup* or *a cup*
'alam	means *pencil* or *a pencil*

The Arabic equivalent of the English definite article is the prefix l-. The definite article precedes the noun and remains unchanged whether the noun is masculine, feminine, singular or plural. The prefix has the form l- if the first consonant of the word to which it is attached is one of the following:

f b m w k g y x G q h " H ', for example:

lbaab	the door
lHammaam	the bathroom

The l- is completely assimilated, resulting in a double consonant, if the first consonant is one of the following:

t T d D s S z Z š n l r, for example:

nnaas	the people
TTayyaara	the plane

At the beginning of a new sentence or after a pause in conversation, this prefix may be preceded by a short 'i, for example:

'issayyaara	the car
'ilyoom	the day

ADJECTIVES

Adjectives in Arabic typically have three forms: masculine, feminine, and plural. The feminine is formed from the masculine by adding -e/-a, for example:

masculine	feminine	
mabSuuT	**mabSuuTa**	well
mniiH	**mniiHa**	good
rxiiS	**rxiiSa**	cheap

Frequently the feminine is formed from a different underlying form, for example:

masculine	feminine	
HaaDir	**HaaDra**	ready
mit'assif	**mit'assfe**	sorry

PLURALS

Most nouns and adjectives have three grammatical numbers: singular, denoting one individual of the kind; dual, denoting two individuals, and plural, denoting more than two individuals. Arabic noun and adjective plurals differ from the corresponding English forms in two principal ways: the plural usually sounds quite different from the singular, and the form of the plural is usually not predictable.

The standard plural is formed by adding suffixes to the singular noun. For masculine nouns and adjectives add -iin, for example:

SuHufi	**SuHufiyyiin**	journalist
mašGuul	**mašGuuliin**	busy

For feminine nouns add -aat, for example:

maHall	**maHallaat**	place
maTaar	**maTaaraat**	airport
'uteel	**uteelaat**	hotel

A large number of Arabic nouns and adjectives have irregular plurals. These plurals have the same root as the singular, but a different pattern, for example:

beet	**buyuut**	house
muftaaH	**mafatiiH**	key
yoom	**'ayyaam**	day

The irregular plural forms are more common than the standard plural. The examples above are for illustration; for complete listings, see the dictionary.

COLLECTIVES

Arabic has a class of nouns called collectives. These nouns indicate a category, not an individual object. The collective form is extremely useful for the tourist since it mainly concerns food, for example:

mooz	bananas
beeD	eggs

The singular form is formed from the collective by the addition of -a, and the plural is usually formed by adding -aat, for example:

baTTiix	watermelons
baTTiixa	a watermelon
tlat baTTiixaat	three watermelons

NOUN-ADJECTIVE AGREEMENT

Adjectives are tied to the nouns they modify by a system of agreement. With masculine nouns the adjective is masculine; with feminine nouns it is feminine. With plurals denoting human beings, the adjective is plural, for example:

'ana mit'assif	*male speaking* I'm sorry.
'ana mit'assfe	*female speaking* I'm sorry.
zuwwaar fransaawiyyiin	French visitors

With non-personal plurals the adjective is usually feminine singular, for example:

'uteelaat jdiide	new hotels

In a noun-adjective construction the adjective follows the noun. If the noun is definite the adjective also has the prefix for *the*, for example:

lbaab lmaftuuH	the open door

NOUN ANNEXION

A frequent construction in Arabic is one consisting of two or more nouns in a closely-knit arrangement called annexion. The annexion phrase is the equivalent of various constructions in English: constructions with the possessive, as in *the girl's age*; constructions with *of*, expressing a similar relation, as in *the age of the girl*; noun phrases, as in the *house-key* (lit. the key of the house).

Phrases with *of* are formed as follows:

noun (possessed) + article l' + noun (possessor), for example:

"unwaan lmat"am	the address of the hotel

Feminine nouns appear in the construct form, that means that -e/-a becomes -it, for example: maktabe *library* + mudiir *director* becomes maktabit lmudiir *the director's library*.

To make the phrase indefinite, simply omit the article, for example:

ša'fit 'maaš   a piece of cloth

The rule is the same for proper nouns, for example:

sayyaarit 'aHmad   Ahmad's car

SENTENCES WITHOUT VERBS

There is no equivalent to the present tense of the verb *to be* in Arabic. Therefore Arabic sentences of the following type do not have any element corresponding to English *is, am, are*.

kiif Haalak?	How are you?
'ana mabSuuT	I am well (personal pronoun + adjective only)
niHna mabSuuTiin	We are well (personal pronoun + adjective only)

PERSONAL PRONOUNS

Arabic has the following set of personal pronouns:

'ana	I (m, f)
'inte	you (m)
'inti	you (f)
huwwe	he
hiyye	she
niHna	we
'intu	you (pl)
humme	they

There is no pronoun corresponding to English *it*. The independent pronouns are not used so much in Arabic as are the corresponding forms in English. They are used mainly as subjects of sentences without verbs, to prevent possible ambiguities, and to add emphasis.

POSSESSIVE PRONOUNS

Arabic has a set of possessive pronouns that occur as suffixes. They are added directly to a masculine noun:

noun +-i	**beeti**	my house
noun +-ak	**beetak**	your (m) house
noun +-ik	**beetik**	your (f) house
noun +-o	**beeto**	his house
noun +-ha	**beetha**	her house
noun +-na	**beetna**	our house
noun +-kum	**beetkum**	your (pl) house
noun +-hum	**beethum**	their house

The feminine -e/-a ending is transformed to -it before adding the possessive suffix, for example:

šanta	**šantiti**	my suitcase

DEMONSTRATIVE PRONOUNS

The demonstrative pronouns are:

haada	this (m)
haadi	this (f)
hadool	these (pl)

They must agree in number and gender with the noun they are replacing and precede it in a sentence, for example:

haada ktaab	this book
haadi lxaarTa	this map

VERBS

The structure of the Arabic verb is very different from English. In theory it is very logical, in practice, especially because of many irregular forms, it can be very difficult. Every Arabic verb has a root consisting of three consonants or vowels that carries a basic meaning. To this are added prefixes and suffixes that add further information about the tense and the doer of the action. The Arabic verb has two tenses: a prefix tense, having subject markers in the form of prefixes, and a suffix tense, having subject markers in the form of suffixes.

The prefix tense usually indicates present or future time, for example:

'aruuH	I go
truuH	you (m) go
truuHi	you (f) go
yruuH	he goes
truuH	she goes
nruuH	we go
truuHu	you (pl) go
yruuHu	they go

The suffix tense usually indicates past time:

fhimt	I understood
fhimt	you (m) understood
fhimti	you (f) understood
fihim	he understood
fihmat	she understood
fhimna	we understood
fhimtu	you (pl) understood
fihmu	they understood

For the reasons given above, the most likely needed forms in conversation will be given in the Arabic phrases.

NEGATION

The word maa *not* is used with verbs and a few other verb-like words, for example:

maa fhimt	I didn't understand.
maa ba"raf	I don't know.

The word miš *not* is used only with adjectives and adverbs, for example:

huwwe miš mabSuuT   He's not well.

huwwe miš hoon   He's not here.

THE WORD BIDD-

The word bidd- *want* combines with pronoun endings to produce the following forms:

biddi	I want
biddak	you (m) want
biddik	you (f) want
biddo	he wants
bidha	she wants
bidna	we want
bidkum	you (pl) want
bidhum	they want

This word, in spite of its verbal meaning, is not a verb in terms of Arabic grammar. Its negative is maa: maa biddi *I don't want*, maa bidna *we don't want*.

THE WORD FII

The word fii *there is, there are* is not a verb in terms of Arabic grammar, in spite of its meaning. Its negative form is maa fii, *there isn't, there aren't*, for example:

maa fii mat"am hoon   There isn't any restaurant here.

QUESTIONS

In Arabic the word order of a question is identical to that of the corresponding statement, for example:

'ijiit fiTTayyaara?   Did you come by plane? (lit.: You came by plane?)

Interrogative words such as feen *where*, 'eemta *when*, 'eeš *what* are usually placed at the end of a question. They do, however, also occur at the beginning, sometimes for emphasis, for example:

feen lmHaTTa? *or*   Where is the station?
  'ilmHaTTa feen?

THE WORD "IND

The word "ind *in the possession of*, in the sense of English *have*, combines with pronoun endings to produce the following forms:

"indi	I have
"indak	you (m) have
"indik	you (f) have
"indo	he has
"indha	she has
"indna	we have
"indkum	you (pl) have
"indhum	they have

The negative is maa or maa fii, for example:

maa fii "indi wlaad   I haven't any children.

THE WORD NŠAALLA

The word nšaalla (lit.: If God wills) indicates that the speaker hopes that something has turned out favorably, or will turn out favorably. When used in a question, the sentence frequently has the intonation of the specific question, with the voice high on the word nšaalla.

NUMBERS

The Arabic counting system differs from English in the following ways:

(1) A noun by itself means *one*, though it may be followed by waaHad *one* (m), waHde *one* (f), according to its gender, for example:

walad waaHid	*one boy*
bint waHde	*one girl*

(2) The noun plus the ending -een means two, for example:

waldeen   *two boys*

binteen   *two girls*

(3) Immediately following the numbers 3-10 the noun is plural.

(4) Immediately following any other numbers the noun is singular.

(5) The numbers from 3-19 have one form when they are used independently and a variant form when they immediately precede a counted noun: 3-10 lose the ending -e/-a, for example: sitte *six*, sitt wlaad *six children*; 11-19 add -ar: sitt ta9š *sixteen*, sitt ta9šar sane *sixteen years*.

EASTERN ARABIC-ENGLISH

The Arabic-English vocabulary is arranged according to the following order:

’ a b d D e f g G h H i j k l m n o q r s S š t T u v w x y z Z “ .

Verbs are entered in the third person masculine singular of the suffix (past) tense, followed by the third person masculine singular of the prefix (present or future) tense, as is customary in most Arabic dictionaries.

Nouns are entered in the singular, followed by the plural, if any.

Adjectives are entered in the masculine singular, followed by the feminine singular, and the plural, if any.

'

’aab	August
’aaDaar	March
’aal bi’uul	to say
’aam bi’uum	to get up
’ab ’abayaat or ’aabaa’	father
’abadan	(not) at all; never
’abil	before; ago
’abyaD beeDa (f) **biiD** (pl)	white
’addeeš	how much; how long
’adiim ’adiime (f) **’a’dam**	old; ancient
’afandi	effendi (a term of address)
’afandi (coll)	tangerines
’ahil (pl)	family
’ahlan wa sahlan	welcome!
’ahwe	coffee
~ **’ahaawi** (pl)	coffee shop
~ **saada**	black coffee without sugar

'aHmar Hamra (f) **Humur** (pl)	red
'aHsan	better; best
'aHyaanan	sometimes
'aja biiji	to come
'ajnabi 'ajnabiyye (f) **ajaanib** (pl)	foreigner
'akal byaakul	to eat
'akbar kubra (f)	bigger, biggest; older, oldest
'akil	food
'akla	dish; meal
'aktar	more; most
'alam 'laam	pencil; pen
'alb	heart
'alf 'aalaaf/taalaaf *or* **'uluuf**	thousand
'aliil 'aliile (f) **'aliiliin** (pl)	small; slight
'alla	God
'amar bu'mur	to order; command
'ameerka	America
'ameerkaani 'ameerkaaniyye (f) **'ameerkaan** (pl)	American
'amiiS 'umSaan	shirt
'amkan bimkin	to be possible
'ana	I
'anniine 'anaani	bottle
'arba"a/'arba"	four
'arD	floor
'arDi šooki (coll)	artichokes

'ariib 'ariibe (f) 'raab (pl)	close; near
~ min	close to
'arnabiiT (coll)	cauliflower
'arye qura	village
'aswad sooda (f) suud (pl)	black
'aSfar Safra (f) Sufur (pl)	yellow
'aSiir 'aSiira (f) 'iSaar (pl)	short
'aSir 'Suur	palace
'ata" bi'ta"	to cut
'aw	or
'awSaT wuSTa (f)	middle; central
'awwal 'uula (f) 'awaa'il (pl)	first
'ax 'ixwe	brother
'axad byaaxud	to take
'axbaar	news
'axDar xaDra (f) xuDur (pl)	green
'ayluul	September
'aywa	yes
'ayy	what; which; any
'ayyaar	May
'azra' zar'a (f) zuru' (pl)	blue
'a"ad bu"ud	to sit down
'a"Ta bya"Ti	to give
'baal	across from
'eemta	when
'eeš	what

'ibin wlaad	son
'ibre 'ubar	needle
'idir bi'dar	to be able
'iid 'ayaadi	hand
'ideen	two hands
'illa	except; minus
'illi	that; which; who; the one
'imm (f) immayaat	mother
'imsaak	constipation
'influwenza	influenza
'ingliizi ingliiziyye (f)	English
'ingliiz (pl)	
'inno	that; that he
'inte	you (m)
'inti	you (f)
'intu	you (pl)
'iri bi'ra	to read
'irš 'ruuš	piastre (monetary unit)
'ishaal	diarrhea
'isim 'asmaa'	name
'iza	if
'izaa"a 'izaa"aat	broadcasting; radio station
'izan	then
'reedis (coll)	shrimp
'uddaam	in front of
'ujra	fare
'unSliyye 'unSliyyaat	consulate
'urduni 'urduniyye (f)	Jordanian
'urduniyyiin (pl)	
'usbuu" 'asabii"	week
'ustaaz 'asaatze	teacher
'uteel 'uteelaat	hotel

'uTun	cotton
'uuDa 'uwaD	room
'uxt (f) xawaat	sister

b

ba'aale ba'aalaat	grocery store
ba'duunis (coll)	parsley
baab bwaab	door
baaba Gannuuj	Middle Eastern dish
baamye (coll)	okra
baarid barda (f)	cold
baaS baaSaat	bus
baaxira bawaaxir	ship
bada bibda	to start; begin
badle badlaat	suit
badlit sbaaHa	swimming suit
badri	early
baGšiiš	tipping, tip
bakkiir	early
bala	without
balaaš	no need
balad (f) blaad	town; country
bandoora (coll)	tomatoes
bank bnuuk	bank
banTaloon	pants
bard	coldness; flu
bariid	mail
~ jawwi	airmail
~ msajjal	registered mail
~ "aadi	regular mail
bariiza	dime (monetary unit)

barnaamaj baraamij	program
barra	outside
baskaleet	bicycle
bass	only
basal (coll)	onions
baSiiT baSiiTa (f) **baSiiTiin** (pl)	simple
baTaaTis (coll)	potatoes
baTii'	slow
baTin	belly
baTTaal baTTaale (f) **baTTaaliin** (pl)	bad
baTTiix (coll)	watermelons
ba"at bib"at	to send
ba"d	after
~ **ZZuhur**	afternoon
ba"deen	later on
ba"d	some
ba"rafš	I don't know
beeD (coll)	eggs
been	between
beeruut (f)	Beirut
beet byuut	house
beetinjaan (coll)	eggplants
beet laHim (f)	Bethlehem
bi'i bib'a	to stay
bid-/bidd-	to want
biduun	without
biDDabT	exactly
biira	beer

binni binniyye (f) **binniyyiin** (pl)	brown
bint (f) **banaat**	daughter; girl
birkit sbaaHa	swimming pool
bisilla (coll)	peas
blaad (f)	country; countries
blaaš	free of charge
bluuze bluuzaat	blouse
booSTa booSTaat	post office
bukra	tomorrow
burd'aan (coll)	oranges
bxeer	good
b"iid "an	far from

d

d'ii'a da'aayi'	minute
daafi	warm
daan dineen	ear
daaxil	inside
daayman	always
dabbaan	flies
dabke dabkaat	dabke (a folk dance)
dafa" bidfa"	to pay
dahab	gold
daraje 'uula	first class
~ taanye	economy class
darraaje	motorcycle
dawa (m) **'adwiye**	medicine
dawle duwal	state; nation
dawwar bidawwir	to look for

daxal budxul	to get into; enter
diik dyuuk	rooster
diik Habaš	turkey
diin adyaan	religion
diinaar dananiir	dinar (currency)
diir baalak	take care!
dismašq	Damascus
dinya	world
dirham daraahim	dirham (currency)
dooHa	dizziness
duGri	straight ahead
dukkaan dakaakiin	shop
duktoor dakaatra	doctor
durraa' (coll)	peaches

D

DaaHiy DawaaHi	suburb
Darab 'ibre buDrub 'ibre	to give an injection
Dariibe Daraa'ib	tax
Daruuri	necessary
Deef Dyuuf	guest

f

fa'iir fa'iire (f) **fu'ara** (pl)	poor
faaDi faaDye (f) **faaDyiin** (pl)	free; empty
faatiH faatHa (f)	light (for colors)
faatuura fawaatiir	bill
fajr	dawn

fakka	change
falaafil	Middle Eastern dish
fallaaH fallaaHiin	peasant
fann	art
farše faršaat	bed
faSuulya (coll)	(haricot/runner) beans
fataH biftaH	to open
fawaakih (coll)	fruits
feen	where
fiDDa	silver
fihim bifham	to understand
fii	there is, there are
fii/fii-/fi-	in
fijil (coll)	radishes
filfil (coll)	pepper
filisTiin	Palestine
filisTiini filisTiiniyye (f) filisTiiniyyiin (pl)	Palestinian
film	movie
fils fluus	fils (monetary unit)
finjaan fanajiin	cup
fiSiH	Easter
fiTir	breaking fast
foo'	above
freez (coll)	strawberries
ftakar biftkir	to think
fTuur	breakfast
furSa furaS	vacation; opportunity
fuSTaan faSaTiin	dress
fuul (coll)	dry broad beans
fuuTa fuwaT	napkin; towel

g

garaaj	garage
gumruk gamaarik	customs

G

Gaali Gaalye (f) **Gaalyiin** (pl)	expensive
Gaami Gaamye	dark (for colors)
Gaayim	cloudy
Gada (m)	lunch
GalaT (invariable adj.)	wrong
Gani Ganiyye (f) **'aGniya** (pl)	rich
Garb	west
Gariib	strange
Gasal biGsul	to wash
Gasiil	laundry; wash
Gurfe Guraf	room

h

haada	this (m)
haadi	this (f)
haadi 'ahda (f)	quiet
hadaak	that (m)
hadiik	that (f)
hadiyye hadaaya	gift; present
hadool	these
haloo	hello (on telephone)
hawiyye hawiyyaat	identity card
hayy	here is, here are
heek	thus, so
hiyye	she

hoon	here
humme	they
hunaak	there
huwwe	he

H

Ha"	price
Haa'it lmabkaa	the Wailing Wall
HaaDir HaaDra (f) HaaDriin (pl)	ready; present
Haadis sayyaara	car accident
HaamiD HaamDa (f)	sour
HaamiD (coll)	lemons
Haarr	hot; spicy
Habb biHibb	to like; love
Habbe Hbuub	pill
Had(a)	anyone; someone
HaDirtak	your presence (a formal term of address)
Hafle Haflaat	party
Hajaz biHjiz	to reserve
Hajj	pilgrimage
Hajz	reservation
Haka biHki	to speak
Halab (f)	Aleppo
Haliib	milk
Halla	now
Hallaa' Hallaa'iin	barber
Hammaam Hammaamaat	bath, bathroom
Hamaawa	fever
Haram	sanctuary

Harb lxaliij	the Gulf War
Hariir	silk
Harkit seer	traffic
Hassaasiyye	allergy
Hatt biHutt	to put
Hatta	until
Hawaali	about, approx.
Hayaa(h) (f)	life
Hayawaan	animal
Hayawaanaat	
Hda"š/Hda"šar	eleven
Hilawiyaat	sweets
Hilu Hilwe (f)	sweet; nice
Hilwiin (pl)	
Hsaab	bill; account
Htaaj biHtaaj	to need
Hubb	love
Hukuume Hukuumaat	government
Hummus (coll)	chickpeas
Hzaam	belt
Hzeeraan	June

j

jaab bijiib	to bring
jaaf	dry
jaahiz jahza (f)	ready
jahziin (pl)	
jaaj	chicken
jaami" jawaami"	mosque
jaam(i)"a jaam(i)"aat	university
jaay jaaye (f)	coming, having come
jaayiin (pl)	

jakeet jake(e)taat	jacket
jamal jmaal	camel
jamb	next to
jamboon	ham
januub	south
januub Garb	southwest
januub šar'	southeast
jariide jaraa'id	newspaper
jawaaz safar	passport
jawla jawlaat	tour
jazar (coll)	carrots
jaziira jazaa'ir	island
jdiid jdiide (f) **jdaad** (pl)	new
jeeš jyuuš	army
jibne	cheese
jiddan	very
jinsiyye	nationality
jneeh jneehaat	pound (currency)
jooz jwaaz	husband
jurH jruu/h	wound
juzdaan	wallet
ju"aan ju"aane (f) **jiyaa"** (pl)	hungry

k

kaan	to be (past tense)
kaanuun (l)'awwal	December
kaanuun (t)taani	January
kaas kaasaat	glass
kaaš	cash
kabbuut kabaabiit	coat

kafitiirya	cafeteria
kahrabe	electricity
kakaaw (f)	hot chocolate
kalb klaab	dog
kalsaat (pl)	socks
kalsoon kalsoonaat	underwear
kam	how many; some; a few
kamaan	also, too
kamara kamaraat	camera
kammuun	cumin
karaz (coll)	cherries
kariim kariime (f) **kurama** (pl)	generous
karm kruum	vineyard; orchard
kart master, visa	Master-, Visa card
kart boostaal	postcard
kasir ksuur	fracture
kaslaan kaslaane (f) **kasaala** (pl)	lazy
katab buktub	to write
kawi	ironing, pressing
kbiir kbiire (f) **kbaar** (pl)	big; old (person)
kibde	liver
kibriit	matches
kifaaye	enough
kiif	how
~ **Haalak?**	*to a male* How are you?
~ **Haalik?**	*to a female* How are you?
kiilo kilowaat	kilo
kiis 'akyaas	(plastic) bag; sack
kilme kilmaat	word

kniise kanaayis	church
kniisit li'yaama	Church of the Holy Sepulchre
kniisit lmahid	Church of the Nativity in Bethlehem
ktaab kutub	book
ktiir	much; a lot; too much
kufte	meat balls
kuHuul	alcohol
kull	all; every
~ **yoom**	every day
kundara kanaadir	pair of dress shoes
kurat lqadam	soccer
kursi karaasi	chair
kwayyis kwayyse (f) **kwayysiin** (pl)	good; fine

l

l'aHad	Sunday
l'arba"a	Wednesday
l'uds (f)	Jerusalem
l'urdun	Jordan
la'	no
laa	no; not
laakin	but
laazim laazme (f) **laazmiin** (pl)	necessary
laban	yogurt
lahje lahjaat	dialect
laHHaam	butcher
laHim laHme	meat
laHmit ba'ar	beef

laHmit xanziir	pork
laHmit xaruuf	lamb
laHmit "ijiil	veal
laHZa min faDlak	a moment, please!
leele layaali	night
leele sa"iide	good night
lleele	tonight
leemuun (coll)	lemons
leeš	why; because
lHa'ii'a	the truth; in fact
lHamdilla	praise be to God
li'anno	because
libis bilbas	to put on; wear
lift (coll)	turnips
liira liiraat	pound (currency)
liista liistaat	menu
ljum"a	Friday
llid	Lod
lmasiiH	Christ
lmasjid l'aqSa	the Aqsa Mosque
loon 'alwaan	color
looz (coll)	almonds
lqaahira	Cairo
lqur'aan	the Koran
lubnaan	Lebanon
lubnaani lubnaaniyye (f) **lubnaaniyyiin** (pl)	Lebanese
luGa luGaat	language
luGit lfuSHa	classical Arabic
luGit l"aammiyye	colloquial Arabic
luubya (coll)	(French) beans
lxamiis	Thursday

m

m'aSS m'aSSaat	scissors
m'addas m'addasse (f) m'addasiin (pl)	holy
ma'kuulaat (pl)	things to eat
ma'li ma'liyye (f)	fried
maa	not
maaDi maaDye (f)	past; last
maaši maašye (f) maašyiin (pl)	walking
maaši lHaal	so-so
mabruuk	congratulations!
mabSuuT mabSuuTa (f) mabSuuTiin (pl)	well
madiine mudun	city
madrase madaaris	school
madxal madaaxil	entrance
maDbuuT maDbuuTa (f)	correct
mafra' mafaari'	cross roads
maftuuH maftuuHa (f)	open
maHall maHallaat	store
~ malaabis	clothing store
maHrame maHaarim	handkerchief
maHši maHšiyye (f)	stuffed
~ maHaaši	stuffed vegetable
majalle majallaat	magazine
majmuu" majmuu"aat	total
makaan 'amkine	place
maktab makaatib	office
~ lbariid	post office
maktabe maktabaat	bookstore; library
maktuub makaatiib	letter

malaabis	clothes
malfuuf (coll)	cabbage
malyaan malyaane (f)	full
malyoon malayiin	million
mamnuu"	forbidden
manTi'a manaaTi'	area
maqluube	Palestinian dish
mara niswaan	wife; woman
maraD 'amraaD	disease
marHaba	hello; welcome
marHabteen	hello (in reply)
mariiD mariiDa (f) **marDa** (pl)	sick
marra	once
marraat	sometimes
mas'ale masaa'il	problem; issue
masa	evening
~ lxeer	good evening
~ nnuur	good evening (in reply)
masiiHi masiiHiyye (f) **masiiHiyyiin** (pl)	Christian
maskiin maskiine (pl) **masakiin** (pl)	poor; unfortunate
masluu' masluu'a (f)	boiled
masmuuH	allowed
masraH	theater
maSari	money
maSir (f)	Egypt
maša bimši	to walk
mašGuul mašGuule (f) **mašGuuliin** (pl)	busy
mašruub mašruubaat	alcoholic beverages

mašwi mašwiyye (f)	broiled
matalan	for example
matHaf mataaHif	museum
maTaar maTaaraat	airport
maTbax maTaabix	kitchen
maT"am maTaa"im	restaurant
maw'if mawaa'if	stopping place
mawjuud mawjuude (f) mawjuudiin (pl)	present; available
maw"id mawaa"id	appointment
maxluuT maxluuTa	mixed
maxraj	exit
mayy (f)	water
mazze	appetizers
ma"	with
~ sslaame	good-by
ma"ak	you (m) have
ma"uul ma"uule (f)	reasonable
ma"aleš	it doesn't matter
ma"diyye	ferry
ma"karoona	macaroni
ma"la'a ma"aali'	spoon
ma"luumaat	information
ma" miin	with whom?
mbaariH	yesterday
mHammar mHammara (f)	roasted
mHaTTa mhaTTaat	station
mijjawwiz mijjawwze (f) mijjawwziin (pl)	married
miin	who; whom; whose
miina (m) mawaani	harbor; port

miliH	salt
min/min-/minn-/mni-	from; than
min faDlak	please *to a male, speaker requesting something*
min faDlik	please *to a female, speaker requesting something*
min ween	from where?
mislim misilme (f) **misilmiin** (pl)	Moslem
mista''jil mista''ijle (f) **mista''ijliin** (pl)	in a hurry
miš	not
~ **baTTaal**	not bad
~ **heek**	isn't it so?
mišmiš (coll)	apricots
miš muhimm	it doesn't matter
mit'assif mit'assfe (f) **mit'assfiin** (pl)	sorry
mit'axxir mit'axxra (f) **mit'axxriin** (pl)	late
mitil	like, similar to
miyye/miit/mit-	hundred
miit 'alf	one hundred thousand
miteen	two hundred
mi''de	stomach
mluxiyye	Jewish mallow (Middle Eastern dish)
mneen (short form of **min ween**)	from where?
mniiH mniiHa (f) **mnaaH** (pl)	good
mooz (coll)	bananas

msaafir msaafriin (pl)	traveler
msakkar msakkara (f)	closed
muftaaH mafatiiH	key
muhimm muhimme (f) **muhimmiin** (pl)	important
mukaalame tilifooniyye	phone call
mukassar mukassra (f)	broken
mumkin	possible
muntazah muntazahaat	park
musalsal musalsalaat	TV show; soap opera
mustaHiil	impossible
mustašfa (m) **mustašfayaat**	hospital
muškile mašaakil	problem
muusiiqa	music
muxtaar maxatiir	headman of a village
m"allim m"allime (f) **m"allmiin** (pl)	teacher

n

naam binaam	to sleep
naar	fire
naas (pl)	people
naašif naašfe	dry
naayim nayme (f) **naaymiin** (pl)	sleeping
naazil nazle (f) **naazliin** (pl)	staying
nabi	prophet
nafs	self; soul; same
~ lwa't	the same time
najme njuum	star

naZZaf binaZZif	to clean
naZZaaraat	glasses
na"am	yes
na"na"	mint
nbiid	wine
nhaar	daytime
nihaaye	end
niHna	we
niisaan	April
nisi binsa	to forget
niswaan (pl)	women; wives
nizil binzil	to land; step down; register at a hotel
njaaS (coll)	pears
noo" 'anwaa"	sort
nšaalla	if God wills
numra numar	number
nusxa nusax	copy
nuSS nSaaS	half; middle
nuur 'anwaar	light
nZiif nZiife (f) **nZaaf** (pl)	clean

q

qaamuus qawaamiis	dictionary
qiTaar	train
qubbit SSaxra	the Dome of the Rock

r

ra's	dancing
raabi"a raab"a	fourth

raadyo	radio
raahib ruhbaan	monk
raaH biruuH	to go
raaHa	rest
raaji" raaj"a (f) **raaj"iin** (pl)	returning
raakib raakbe (f) **raakbiin** (pl)	riding
raas ruus	head
raayiH raayHa (f) **raayHiin** (pl)	going
rabii"	spring
rajul rjaal	man
ramaadi ramaadiyye (f)	gray
ramil	sand
raqam 'arqaam	number
rašiH	a cold
riHle riHlaat	journey; trip
riji" birja" (min)	to return (from)
rikib birkab	to ride
riyaaDa	sport
rubu" rbaa"	quarter
rukbe rukab	knee
rušeeta	prescription
ruzz	rice
rxiiS rxiiSa (f)	inexpensive

s

sa'al bis'al	to ask
saa' bisuu'	to drive
saada (invariable adj.)	plain

saabii" saab"a	seventh
saadis saadse	sixth
saafar bisaafir	to travel
saaHa saaHaat	courtyard
saaHil	shore
saakin saakne (f) saakniin (pl)	dwelling
saami saam"a (f) saam"iin (pl)	hearing
saayiH saayHiin	tourist
saari saarye (f)	contagious
saa"a saa"aat	hour; watch
~ mnabbih	alarm clock
saa"ad bisaa"id	to help
sabaanix (coll)	spinach
sabaH bisbaH	to swim
sab"a ta"š/saba" ta"šar	seventeen
sab"a/sabi"/sab"	seven
sab"iin	seventy
safaara safaaraat	embassy
safar	travel
safra safraat	trip
sahra sahraat	evening party
sakan buskun	to dwell
sakkar bisakkir	to close
salaam	peace
'assalaamu "alaykum	the peace upon you
salaame	safety
sama	sky
samak (coll)	fish
sanduu' sanadii'	box
sane sniin	year

sarii"	fast
sawa	together
sayyaara sayyaaraat	car
sayyid	Mr.
sa"iid sa"iide (f) su"ada (pl)	happy
sbaaHa	swimming
sihil	easy
siigaara sagaayir	cigarette
sikkit Hadiid	railway
sikkiin sakakiin	knife
simi" bisma"	to hear
sinama	movie theater
sinn snaan	tooth
sitte/sitt	six
sittiin	sixty
sitt ta"š/sitt ta"šar	sixteen
siyaaHa	tourism
siyaase	politics
si"ir 'as"aar	price
ssabt	Saturday
ssu"uudiyye	Saudi Arabia
stanna bistanna	to wait
staraaH bistriiH	to rest
su'aal 'as'ile	question
sukkar	sugar
suu' (f) aswaa'	market
suur	wall
suuriyya	Syria
su"aal	coughing
sxuuune	fever

S

Saabuun	soap
SaaHib ('a)SHaab	friend; owner
SabaaH	morning
~ **lxeer**	good morning
~ **nnuur**	good morning (in reply)
Sabi Subyaan	boy; child
Sadii' 'aSdi'aa'	friend
SaHiiH	correct
SaHin SHuun	plate
SalaTa SalaTaat	salad
SallaH biSalliH	to repair
Saraf biSruf	to cash; spend; change money
Sarraaf	money-changer
Saydaliyye	pharmacy
Sa"b	difficult
Seef	summer
SGiir SGiire (f) **SGaar** (pl)	small; young
Sifir	zero
SiHHa	health
SiHHi SiHHiyye	healthy
Suddaa"	headache
Suuf	wool
Suura Suwar	picture

š

ša'fe šu'af	piece
šaaf bišuuf	to look; see
šaami šaamiyye (f) **šwaam** (pl)	Syrian; Damascene

šaari" šawaari"	street
šaaTir šaTra (f) šaTriin (pl)	clever
šaay	tea
šaayif šaayfe (f) šaayfiin (pl)	looking; seeing
šahir 'ašhur/tušhur	month
šajar	tree
šakar buškur	to thank
šamandar (coll)	beets
šams	sun
šanta šonat	bag
šarii"a	religious law of Islam
šar'	east
šar' l'awSaT	the Middle East
šaTT lbaHar	beach
šarwirma	Middle Eastern dish
šaxS 'ašxaaS	person
ša"b	people
ša"ir	hair
šbaaT	February
šeex šyuux	sheikh
šibšib	slippers
šii 'ašya(a')	thing; something
šiis kebaab	Middle Eastern dish
šimmaal	north
~ Garb	northwest
~ šar'	northeast
šimmaam (coll)	melon
širib bišrab	to drink
širkit Tayraan	airline
šita (m)	winter

šmaal	left (side)
šoob	heat
šooke suwak	fork
šooraba	soup
ššaam (f)	Damaskus
štaGal bištGil	to work
štara bištri	to buy
šubbaak šababiik	window
šukran	thank you
šuu	what
~ **maalo?**	what's wrong with him?
šwayy (f)	a little bit
šwayyit sukkar	a little bit of sugar
šwayy, šwayy	slowly

t

ti'iil ti'iile (f) **t'aal** (pl)	heavy
ta'miin	insurance
ta'riiban	approximately
taajir tujjaar	merchant
taali	following
taalit taalte	third
taamin taamne	eighth
taani taanye	second; other
taarix tawaariix	history; date
taasi" taas"a	ninth
tabbuule	Middle Eastern dish
tadfi'a	heating
taHt	under
takyiif	air-conditioning
talabbuk mi"de	upset stomach

talfan bitalfin	to call s.o. by phone
talj	ice
tamaanye/taman/tamn	eight
tamaniin	eighty
taman taʿš/taman taʿšar	eighteen
tammuuz	July
tanZiif	cleaning
tannuura tananiir	skirt
tarak bitrik or butruk	to leave
tarjame tarjamaat	translation
taSliiH	repairing
taxt txuute	bed
~ **mifrid**	twin bed
~ **mijwiz**	double bed
tazkare tazaakir	ticket
~ **raayiH bass**	one-way ticket
~ **raayiH jayy**	round-trip ticket
taʿaal	come!
taʿbaan taʿbaane (f) taaʿbaaniin (pl)	tired
tfaDDal	please to a male, speaker offering something
tfaDDali	please to a female, speaker requesting something
tfaDDal striiH	please sit down
tfaDDal maʿi	please come with me
tiin (coll)	figs
tisiʿ taʿš/tisiʿ taʿšar	nineteen
tisʿa/tisiʿ/tisʿ	nine
tisʿiin	ninety

tišriin (l)'awwal	October
tišriin (t)taani	November
tlaate/tlaat/tlat	three
tlaatiin	thirty
tlat ta"š/tlat ta"šar	thirteen
tna"š/tna"šr	twelve
tneen tinteen (f)	two
tšarrafna	nice to meet you
ttlaata	Tuesday
ttineen	Monday
tuffaaH (coll)	apples
tult tlaat	third
tuum (coll)	garlic
tuut (coll)	mulberries
t"ašša bit"ašša	to dine

T

Ta'S	weather; climate
Taabi' Tawaabi'	floor; story
Taabi" Tawaabi"	stamp
Taalib Tullaab (pl)	student
Taawle Taawlaat	table
Taaza (invariable adj.)	fresh
Tab"an	of course
Tamir (coll)	dates
Taraablus (f)	Tripoli
Tarii' Turu'	road; way
Tawiil Tawiile (f) **Tiwaal** (pl)	long
Tayyaara Tayyaaraat	airplane
Tayyib Tayybe (f) **Tayybiin** (pl)	good; tasty

Tayyib	all right
Tbiib	physician
Teer Tyuur	bird
THiina	oil of sesame seeds
Tifil 'aTfaal	child

w

w-/wi-	and; when; while
wa"f biwa"if	to stop
wa't	time
waa'if waa'fe (f) **waa'fiin** (pl)	standing; stopping; stopped
waadi widyaan	valley
waaHad waHde (f)	one
waaHad, waaHad	one by one
waalde waaldaat	mother
waalid waaldiin	father
waja" wjaa"	pain; ache
~ **baTin**	stomach ache
~ **mi"de**	stomach ache
~ **raas**	headache
~ **snaan**	toothache
wakaale wakaalaat	agency
wala šii	nothing
walad wlaad	boy
walla or **wallaahi**	by God
wara' war'aat	sheet of paper, paper
~ **"inab**	vine leaves
wara	behind
waSaT	center
ween	where

wilaaye wilaayaat	state; province
lwilaayaat lmuttáHide	the United States
willa	or
wiSil biyuuSal	to arrive
wusix wusxa (f)	dirty
wusxiin (pl)	

x

xaaf bixaaf (min)	to be afraid (of)
xaamis xaamse (f)	fifth
xaarTa xaraayiT	map
xabar 'axbaar	news
xabbaaz	baker
xadd xduud	cheek
xafiif xafiife (f)	light (of weight)
xfaaf (pl)	
xamir	wine
xamse/xamis/xams	five
xamsiin	fifty
xams taʿš/xams taʿšar	fifteen
xarbaan xarbaane (f)	out of order
xariif	fall, autumn
xariiTa xaraayiT	map
xaruuf xirfaan	lamb
xaSim	discount
xaSS (coll)	lettuce
xeeme xeemaat	tent
xeeD	thread
xidme	service
xiTTa xiTTat	plan
xoox (coll)	plums

xubz	bread
xuDra	vegetables
xyaar (coll)	cucumbers

y

yaa	particle of address and exclamation
yaa siidi	Sir
yahuudi yahuudiyye (f) **yahuud** (pl)	Jew; Jewish
yamiin	right (side)
ya"ni	it means; that is; well ...; more or less; for instance
yoom ('a)yyaam/tiyyaam	day
lyoom	today
yuusif 'afandi (coll)	tangerines

z

zaar bizuur	to visit
zaayir zaayre (f) **zaayriin** (pl)	visiting
zahar (coll)	cauliflower
zakaat	almsgiving
zamaan	long ago
zayy maa biddak	as you (m sg) wish
zbaale	garbage
zbuun zbaayin	customer
zeet	oil
zeetuun (coll)	olives
zibde	butter
zirr zraar	button

zooj zwaaj	husband
zooje zoojaat	wife

Z

Zann biZunn	to suppose; think; believe
Zarf Zruuf	envelope
Zuhur	noon

"

"aadatan	usually
"aadi "aadiyye (f) **"aadiyyiin** (pl)	regular; ordinary
"aalam	world
"aali "aalye (f)	high
"aam	year
"aašir "aašre	tenth
"adad 'a"daad	number
"afwan	you're welcome (in reply to *sukran*)
"ala/"alee/"alay/"a-	to; on; incumbent upon
"ala yamiinak	to your right
"amal	work
"amaliyye	operation; surgery
"ammaan (f)	Amman
"an/"an-/"ann-	about
"ara'	arak (an alcoholic beverage)
"arabi "arabiyye (f) **"arab** (pl)	Arab; Arabic
"aSiir	juice
"aša	dinner
"ašiyye "ašiyyaat	evening

"ašra/"ašar/"ašr	ten
"aZiim "aZiime (f) "uZamaa' (pl)	great; magnificent
"eele "iyal	family
"een (f) "uyuun	eye
"iddit	several
~ marraat	several times
"iid ('a)"yaad	feast day
~ miilaad	birthday
~ lmiilaad	Christmas
~ lfiSiH	Easter
~ raas ssane	New Year's Day
~ lmawlid	birthday of the Prophet
~ lfiTir	breaking of the fast of Ramadan
~ l'aDHa	feast of the Sacrifice
"imil bi"mal	to do; make
"inab (coll)	grapes
"ind/"in-	in the possession of; have
"irif bi"raf	to know
"išriin	twenty
"unwaan "anawiin	address
"urs ' "raas	wedding

ENGLISH-EASTERN ARABIC

A

English	Eastern Arabic
able (be ~ , vb)	'idir bi'dar
about (approx.)	Hawaali
about	"an/"an-/"ann-
above	foo'
adapter	wuSla muhaaya'a
ache	waja" wjaa"
across from	'baal
adhesive bandage	"iSaaba
address	"unwaan "anawiin
afraid, be (of)	xaaf bixaaf (min)
after	ba"d
afternoon	ba"d ZZuhur
again	min jdiid
agency	wakaale wakaalaat
ago	'abil
air-conditioning	takyiif
airline	širkit Tayraan
airplane	Tayyaara Tayaaraat
airport	maTaar maTaaraat
alarm clock	saa"a mnabbih
alcohol	kuHuul
alcoholic beverages	mašruub mašruubaat
Aleppo	Halab (f)
all	kull
allergy	Hassaasiyye
allowed	masmuuH
all right	Tayyib

almonds	looz
almsgiving	zakaat
also	kamaan
always	daayman
ambulance	sayyarit 'is"aaf
America	'ameerka
American	'ameerkaani 'ameerkaaniyye (f) 'ameerkaan (pl)
Amman	"ammaan (f)
ancient	'adiim 'adiime (f) 'a'dam (pl)
and	w-/wi-
animal	Hayawaan Hayawaanaat
antibiotic	'antibiyotik
any	'ayy
anyone	Had(a)
appetizers	mazze
apples	tuffaaH (coll)
appointment	maw"id mawaa"id
approximately	ta'riiban
apricots	mišmiš (coll)
April	niisaan
Aqsa Mosque, the	lmasjid l'aqSa
Arab	"arabi "arabiyye (f) "arab (pl)
Arabic	"arabi
Arabic (classical)	luGit lfuSHa
Arabic (colloquial)	luGit l"aammiyye
arak	"ara'
area	manTi'a manaaTi'

army	jeeš jyuuš
arrive (vb)	wiSil biyuuSal
art	fann
artichokes	'arDi šooki (coll)
as you (m sg) **wish**	zayy maa biddak
ask (vb)	sa'al bis'al
August	'aab
autumn	xariif
available	mawjuud mawjuude (f) mawjuudiin (pl)

B

bad	baTTaal baTTaale (f) baTTaaliin (pl)
not ~	miš baTTaal
bag	šanta šonat
bag (plastic ~)	kiis 'akyaas
baker	xabbaaz
bakery	maxbaz
balcony	balkoona
bananas	mooz (coll)
bank	bank bnuuk
barber	Hallaa' Hallaa'iin
bath, bathroom	Hammaam Hammaamaat
battery	battaariyye
be, to (past tense)	kaan
beach	šaTT lbaHar
beans (dry broad ~)	fuul (coll)
French ~	luubya (coll)
haricot ~	faSuulya (coll)
because	leeš; li'anno

bed	farše faršaat; taxt txuute
double ~	taxt mijwiz
twin ~	taxt mifrid
beef	laHmit ba'ar
beer	biira
beets	šamandar (coll)
before	'abil
begin (vb)	bada bibda
behind	wara
Beirut	beeruut (f)
believe (vb)	Zann biZunn
belly	baTin
belt	Hzaam
best	'aHsan
Bethlehem	beet laHim (f)
better	'aHsan
between	been
bicycle	baskaleet
big	kbiir kbiire (f) kbaar (pl)
bigger; biggest	'akbar kubra (f)
bill	faatuura; Hsaab
birthday	"iid miilaad
black	'aswad sooda (f) suud (pl)
black coffee **without sugar**	'ahwe saada
blanket	Hraam
blood	dam
~ group	zumra damawiyye
~ pressure	DaGt damawi
~ transfusion	na'l dam
blouse	bluuze bluuzaat
blue	'azra' zar'a (f) zuru' (pl)

boiled	masluu' masluu'a (f)
book	ktaab kutub
bookstore	maktabe maktabaat
bottle	'anniine 'anaani
box	Sanduu' Sanadii'
boy	walad wlaad; Sabi Subyaan
bracelet	suwaar
brass	nuHaas 'aSfar
bread	xubz
breakfast	fTuur
breaking fast	fiTtir
bring (vb)	jaab bijiib
broadcasting	'izaa"a 'izaa"aat
broiled	mašwi mašwiyye (f)
broken	mukassar mukassra (f)
brother	'ax 'ixwe
brown	binni binniyye (f) binniyyiin (pl)
bus	baaS baaSaat
busy	mašGuul mašGuule (f) mašGuuliin (pl)
but	laakin
butcher	laHHaam
butter	zibde
button	zirr zraar
buy (vb)	štara bištri
by God	walla *or* wallaahi

C

cabbage	malfuuf (coll)
cafeteria	kafitiirya
Cairo	lqaahira

call s.o. by phone (vb)	talfan bitalfin
camel	jamal jmaal
camera	kamara kamaraat
car	sayyaara sayyaaraat
~ **accident**	haadis sayyara
carpet	sijaade
carrots	jazar (coll)
cash	kaaš
cash (vb)	Saraf biSruf
cauliflower	'arnabiiT; zahar (coll)
cemetery	ma'bare
center	waSaT; markaz
central	awSaT wuSTa (f)
chair	kursi karaasi
change	fakka
change money (vb)	Saraf biSruf
check	šek
cheek	xadd xduud
cheese	jibne
cherries	karaz (coll)
chicken	jaaj
chickpeas	Hummus (coll)
Christ	lmasiiH
Christian	masiiHi masiiHiyye (f) masiiHiyyiin (pl)
Christmas	"iid lmiilaad
church	kniise kanaayis
Church of the Holy Sepulchre	kniisit li'yaama
Church of the Nativity in Bethlehem	kniisit lmahid
cigarette	siigaara sagaayir

city	madiine mudun
class	daraje
first ~	daraje 'uula
economy ~	daraje taanye
clean	nZiif nZiife (f) nZaaf (pl)
clean (vb)	naZZaf binaZZif
cleaning	tanZiif
clever	šaaTir šaTra (f)
	šaTriin (pl)
close (vb)	sakkar bisakkir
close (to)	'ariib 'ariibe (f) 'raab (pl)
	(min)
closed	msakkar msakkara (f)
clothes	malaabis
clothing store	maHall malaabis
cloudy	Gaayim
coat	kabbuut kabaabiit
coffee	'ahwe
~ shop	'ahwe 'ahaawi
cold	baarid barda (f)
cold (a ~)	rašiH
color	loon 'alwaan
comb	mišT
come (vb)	'aja biiji
come!	ta"aal
coming, having come	jaay jaaye (f) jaayiin (pl)
command (vb)	'amar bu'mur
congratulations	mabruuk
constipation	'imsaak
consulate	'unSliyye 'unSliyyaat
contact lenses	"adasaat laaSi'a
contagious	saari saarye (f)

copper	nuHaas
copy	nusxa nusax
correct	saHiih; maDbuuT
cotton	'uTun
coughing	su"aal
country	balad (f) blaad
courtyard	saaHa saaHaat
cramp	tašannuj
cross roads	mafra' mafaari'
cucumbers	xyaar (coll)
cumin	kammuun
cup	finjaan fanajiin
customer	zbuun zbaayin
customs	gumruk gamaarik
cut (vb)	'ata" bi'ta"

D

Damascus	dismašq
dancing	ra's
dark (for colors)	Gaami Gaamye
date	taarix tawaariix
dates	tamir
daughter	bint (f) banaat
dawn	fajr
day	yoom ('a)yyaam/tiyyaam
every ~	kull yoom
daytime	nhaar
December	kaanuun (l)'awwal
dentist	duktoor 'asnaan
deodorant	muziil rraa'iHa
diabetes	maraD lbawl ssukari

dialect	lahje lahjaat
diarrhea	'ishaal
dictionary	qaamuus qawaamiis
difficult	sa"b
dime	bariiza
dine (vb)	t"ašša bit"ašša
dinner	"aša
dirty	wusix wusxa (f) wusxiin (pl)
discount	xaSim
disease	maraD 'amraaD
dish	'akla
dizziness	dooHa
do (vb)	"imil bi"mal
doctor	duktoor dakaatra
dog	kalb klaab
Dome of the Rock, the	qubbit SSaxra
door	baab bwaab
dress	fuSTaan faSaTiin
drink (vb)	širib bišrab
drive (vb)	saa' bisuu'
dry	naašif naašfe; jaaf
dwell (vb)	sakan buskun
dwelling	saakin saakne (f) saakniin (pl)

E

ear	daan dineen
early	badri; bakkiir
earrings	Hala'
east	šar'

Easter	fisiH, "iid lfisiH
easy	sihil
eat (vb)	'akal byaakul
eggplants	beetinjaan (coll)
eggs	beeD (coll)
Egypt	maSir (f)
eight	tammanye/taman/tamn
eighteen	taman ta"š/taman ta"šar
eighth	taamin taamne
eighty	tamaniin
electricity	kahrabe
eleven	Hda"š/Hda"šar
enamel	miinaa'
embassy	safaara safaaraat
embroidery	taTriiz
empty	faaDi faaDye (f) faaDyiin (pl)
end	nihaaye
English	'ingliizi ingliiziyye (f) 'ingliiz
enough	kifaaye
enter (vb)	daxal budxul
entrance	madxal madaaxil
envelope	Zarf Zruuf
evening	masa; "ašiyye "ašiyyaat
good ~	masa lxeer
good ~ (in reply)	masa nnuur
~ party	sahra sahraat
every	kull
exactly	biDDabT
example, for	matalan
except	'illa

exchange rate	si"r taHwiil
exhibition	ma"rad
exit	maxraj
expensive	Gaali Gaalye (f)
	Gaalyiin (pl)
eye	"een (f) "uyuun

F

fall	xariif
fan	marwaHa
family	'ahil (pl); "eele "iyal
far (from)	b"iid ("an)
fare	'ujra
fast	sarii"
father	'ab 'abayaat *or* 'aabaa';
	waalid waaldiin
fax	faks
feast day	"iid ('a)"yaad
February	šbaaT
ferry	ma"diyye
fever	Hamaawa; sxuuune
few, a	kam
fifteen	xams ta"š/xams ta"šar
fifth	xaamis xaamse (f)
fifty	xamsiin
figs	tiin (coll)
fine	kwayyis kwayyse (f)
	kwayysiin (pl)
fire	naar
first	'awwal 'uula (f)
	'awaa'il (pl)
fish	samak (coll)

five	xamse/xamis/xams
flies	dabbaan
floor	'arD
floor (story)	Taabi' Tawaabi'
flu	bard
following	taali
food	'akil; ma'kuulaat (pl)
forbidden	mamnuu"
foreigner	'ajnabi 'ajnabiyye (f) ajaanib (pl)
forget (vb)	nisi binsa
fork	šooke šuwak
forty	arb"iin
four	'arba"a/'arba"
fourteen	'arba" ta"š
fourth	raabi"a raab"a
fracture	kasir ksuur
free (empty)	faaDi faaDye (f) faaDyiin (pl)
free of charge	blaaš
fresh	Taaza (invariable adj.)
Friday	ljum"a
fried	ma'li ma'liyye (f)
friend	SaaHib ('a)SHaab (pl); Sadii' 'aSdi'aa'
from	min/min-/minn-/mni-
from where	min ween, mneen
front of, in	'uddaam
fruits	fawaakih (coll)
full	malyaan malyaane (f)

G

garage	garaaj
garbage	zbaale
garlic	tuum (coll)
gas station	maHaTTit benziin
generous	kariim kariime (f) kurama (pl)
germs	jaraatiim
get into (vb)	daxal budxul
get up (vb)	'aam bi'uum
gift	hadiyye hadaaya
girl	bint (f) banaat
give (vb)	'a"ta bya"'ti
give an injection (vb)	Darab 'ibre buDrub ibre
glass	kaas kaasaat
glasses	naZZaaraat
go (vb)	raaH biruuH
God	'alla
going	raayiH raayHa (f) raayHiin (pl)
gold	dahab
good (adj)	bxeer
good	kwayyis kwayyse (f) kwayysiin (pl); mniiH mniiHa (f) mnaaH (pl)
good-bye	ma" sslaame
government	Hukuume Hukuumaat
grapes	"inab (coll)
gray	ramaadi ramaadiyye (f)
great	"aziim "aziime (f) "uzamaa' (pl)

green	'axDar xaDra (f) xuDur (pl)
grocery store	ba'aale ba'aalaat
guest	Deef Dyuuf
Gulf War, the	Harb lxaliij

H

hair	ša"ir
hairbrush	furšit ša"ir
hairdresser	kuwafeer
half	nuSS nSaaS
ham	jamboon
hand	'iid 'ayaadi
two ~s	'ideen
handkerchief	maHrame maHaarim
happy	sa"iid sa"iide (f) su"ada (pl)
harbor	miina (m) mawaani
hat	burneeta
have	"ind/"in-
you (m) ~	ma"ak
he	huwwe
head	raas ruus
headache	Suddaa"; waja" raas
health	siHHa
healthy	SiHHi siHHiyye
hear (vb)	simi" bisma"
hearing	saami" saam"a (f) saam"iin (pl)
heart	'alb
~ attack	nawbe 'albiyye
heat	šoob

heating	tadfi'a
heavy	ti'iil ti'iile (f) t'aal (pl)
hello	marHaba
hello (in reply)	marHabteen
help (vb)	saa"ad bisaa"id
high	"aali "aalye (f)
history	taarix tawaariix
holy	m'addas m'addasse (f) m'addasiin (pl)
hospital	mustašfa (m) mustašfayaat
hot (spicy)	Haarr
hot chocolate	kakaaw (f)
hotel	'uteel 'uteelaat
hour	saa"a saa"aat
house	beet byuut
how	kiif
~ **are you?** (m sg)	kiif Haalak?
~ **are you?** (f sg)	kiif Haalik?
~ **long**	'addeeš
~ **many**	kam
~ **much**	'addeeš
hundred	miyye/miit/mit-
hungry	ju"aan ju"aane (f) jiyaa" (pl)
hurry, in a	mista"jil mista"ijle (f) mista"ijliin (pl)
husband	jooz jwaaz; zooj zwaaj

I

I	'ana
ice	talj
ice cream	buuza

identity card	hawiyye hawiyyaat
if	'iza
important	muhimm muhimme (f) muhimmiin (pl)
impossible	mustaHiil
in	fii/fii-/fi-
in fact	lHa'ii'a
in front of	'uddaaam
in the possession of	"ind/"in-
incumbent upon	"ala/"alee/"alay/"a-
inexpensive	rxiiS rxiiSa (f)
infection	"adwaa
influenza	'influwenza
information	ma"luumaat
inside	daaxil
instance, for	ya"ni
insurance	ta'miin
interpreter	mtarjim
ironing	kawi
island	jaziira jazaa'ir
isn't it so	miš heek
issue	mas'ale masaa'il

J

jacket	jakeet jake(e)taat
January	kaanuun (t)taani
Jerusalem	l'uds (f)
Jew; Jewish	yahuudi yahuudiyye (f) yahuud (pl)
jewelry	mjawharaat

Jordan	l'urdun
Jordanian	'urduni 'urduniyye (f) 'urduniyyiin (pl)
journey	riHle riHlaat
juice	"aSiir
July	tammuuz
June	Hzeeraan

K

key	muftaaH mafatiiH
kilo	kiilo kilowaat
kitchen	maTbax maTaabix
knee	rukbe rukab
knife	sikkiin sakakiin
know (vb)	"irif bi"raf
I don't ~	ba"rafš
Koran, the	lqur'aan

L

lamb (meat)	laHmit xaruuf
land (vb)	nizil binzil
language	luGa luGaat
last	maaDi maaDye (f)
late	mit'axxir mit'axxre (f) mit'axxriin (pl)
later on	ba"deen
laundry	Gasiil
lazy	kaslaan kaslaane (f) kasaala (pl)
leather	jild

leave (vb)	tarak bitrik *or* butruk
Lebanese	lubnaani lubnaaniyye (f) lubnaaniyyiin (pl)
Lebanon	lubnaan
left (side)	šmaal
left, to your	"ala šmaalak
lemons	leemuun; HaamiD (coll)
lentils	"ads
letter	maktuub makaatiib
lettuce	xaSS (coll)
library	maktabe maktabaat
life	Hayaa(h) (f)
light (for colors)	faatiH faatHa (f)
light (of weight)	xafiif xafiife (f) xfaaf (pl)
light	nuur 'anwaar
lighter	'addaaHa
like (vb)	Habb biHibb
like	mitil
little bit, a	šwayy (f)
a little bit of sugar	šwayyit sukkar
liver	kibde
Lod	llid
long ago	zamaan
look (vb)	šaaf bišuuf
look for (vb)	dawwar bidawwir
lose (vb)	xasir bixsar
lot, a	ktiir
love (vb)	Habb biHibb
love	Hubb
lunch	Gada (m)

M

macaroni	ma"karoona
magazine	majalle majallaat
magnificent	"aziim "aziime (f) "uzamaa' (pl)
mail	bariid
air ~	bariid jawwi
registered ~	bariid msajjal
regular ~	bariid "aadi
make (vb)	"imil bi"mal
man	rajul rjaal
map	xaarTa xaraayiT; xariiTa xaraayiT
March	'aadaar
market	suu' (f) aswaa'
married	mijjawwiz mijjawwze (f) mijjawwziin (pl)
matches, box of ~	kibriit
matter, it doesn't	ma"aleeš; miš muhimm
May	'ayyaar
meal	'akla
means, it	ya"ni
meat	laHim, laHme
medicine	dawa (m) 'adwiye
melon	šimmaam (coll)
menu	liista liistaat
merchant	taajir tujjaar
middle	l'awSaT wuSTa (f)
Middle East, the	ššar' l'awSaT
milk	Haliib

million	malyoon malayiin
mint	na"na"
minus	'illa
minute	d'ii'a da'aayi'
mixed	maxluuT maxluuTa
moment	laHZa
a moment please!	laHZa min faDlak
monastery	deer
Monday	(yoom) ttineen
money	maSaari
money-changer	Sarraaf
monk	raaHib ruHbaan
month	šahir 'ašhur/tušhur
monument	'atar
more	'aktar
more or less	ya"ni
morning	SabaaH
good ~	SabaaH lxeer
good ~ (in reply)	SabaaH nnuur
Moslem	mislim misilme (f) misilmiin (pl)
mosque	jaami" jawaami"
most	'aktar
mother	'imm (f) immayaat; waalde waaldaat
motorcycle	darraaje
mountain	jabal
movie theater	sinama
movie	film
Mr.	sayyid
much	ktiir
too ~	ktiir

mulberries	tuut (coll)
museum	matHaf mataaHif
music	muusiiqa

N

name	'isim 'asmaa'
napkin	fuuTa fuwaT
nation	dawle duwal
nationality	jinsiyye
near	'ariib 'ariibe (f) 'raab (pl)
necessary	Daruuri
necessary	laazim laazme (f) laazmiin (pl)
necklace	"iqd
necktie	gravaat
need (vb)	Htaaj biHtaaj
need, no	balaaš
needle	'ibre 'ubar
never	'abadan
new	jdiid jdiide (f) jdaad (pl)
news	'axbaar
newspaper	jariide jaraa'id
newsstand	dukkaan jaraa'id
New Year's Day	"iid raas ssane
next to	jamb
nice	Hilu Hilwe (f) Hilwiin (pl)
nice to meet you	tšarrafna
night	leele layaali
good ~	leele sa"iide
nine	tis"a/tisi"/tis"
nineteen	tisi" ta"š/tisi" ta"šar

ninety	tisʿiin
ninth	taasiʿ taasʿa
no	laa; la'
noon	Zuhur
north	šimmaal
northeast	šimmaal šar'
northwest	šimmaal Garb
not	laa; maa; miš
not at all	'abadan
nothing	wala šii
November	tišriin (t)taani
now	Halla
number	numra numar; raqam 'arqaam; ʿadad 'aʿdaad
nurse	mumarriDa

O

October	tišriin (l)'awwal
office	maktab makaatib
office of tourism	maktab siyaaHa
oil	zeet
okra	baamye (coll)
old (person)	kbiir kbiire (f) kbaar
old	'adiim 'adiime (f) 'a'dam
older; oldest	'akbar kubra (f)
olives	zeetuun (coll)
on	ʿala/ʿalee/ʿalay/ʿa-
once	marra
one	waaHad waHde (f)
one by one	waaHad, waaHad

one hundred thousand	miit 'alf
onions	basal (coll)
only	bass
open (vb)	fataH biftaH
open	maftuuH maftuuHa
operation	"amaliyye
opportunity	furSa furaS
or	'aw; willa
oranges	burd'aan (coll)
orchard	karm kruum
order (vb)	'amar bu'mur
ordinary	"aadi "aadiyye (f) "aadiyyiin (pl)
other	taani taanye (f)
out of order	xarbaan xarbaane (f)
outside	barra
owner	SaaHib ('a)SHaab

P

pain	waja" wjaa"
palace	'aSir 'Suur
Palestine	filisTiin
Palestinian	filisTiini filisTiiniyye (f) filisTiiniyyiin (pl)
pants	banTaloon
paper, sheet of paper	wara' war'aat
park	muntazah muntazahaat
parsley	ba'duunis (coll)
party	Hafle Haflaat
passport	jawaaz safar

past	maaDi maaDye
pay (vb)	dafa" bidfa"
peace	salaam
peaches	durraa'
pears	njaaS (coll)
peas	bisilla (coll)
peasant	fallaaH fallaaHiin
pencil; pen	'alam 'laam
people	naas (pl); ša"b
pepper	filfil (coll)
permission	'izin 'zuune *or* 'uzuunaat
person	šaxS 'ašxaaS
pharmacy	Saydaliyye
phone	tilifoon
~ **call**	mukaalame tilifooniyye
picture	Suura Suwar
piece	ša'fe šu'af
pilgrimage	Hajj
pill	Habbe Hbuub
pipe	biiba
place	makaan 'amkine
plain	saada (invariable adj.)
plan	xiTTa xiTTat
plate	SaHin SHuun
platform	raSiif
please	*to a male, speaker offering something* tfaDDal
	to a female, speaker offering something tfaDDali
	to a male, speaker requesting something min faDlak

	to a female, speaker requesting something min faDlik
~ come with me	tfaDDal ma"i
~ sit down	tfaDDal striiH
plug	sidaade
plums	xoox (coll)
politics	siyaase
poor	fa'iir fa'iire (f) fu'ara (pl)
poor; unfortunate	maskiin maskiina (f) masakiin (pl)
pork	laHmit xanziir
port	miina (m) mawaani
possible (be ~ ,vb)	'amkan bimkin
possible	mumkin
postcard	kart booSTaal
post office	booSTa booSTaat; maktab lbariid
potatoes	baTaaTis (coll)
pottery	faxxaar
pound (currency)	jneeh jneehaat
pregnant	Haamil (f)
prescription	rušeeta
present	HaaDir HaaDra (f) HaaDriin (pl); mawjuud mawjuude (f) mawjuudiin (pl)
pressing	kawi
price	si"ir 'as"aar
problem	mas'ale masaa'il; muškile mašaakil
program	barnaamaj baraamij
prophet	nabi

province	wilaaye wilaayaat
put (vb)	Hatt biHutt
put on (vb)	libis bilbas

Q

quarter	rubu" rbaa"
question	su'aal 'as'ile

R

radio	raadyo
radishes	fijil (coll)
railway	sikkit Hadiid
razor	muusa
read (vb)	'iri bi'ra
ready	jaahiz jahza (f) jahziin (pl)
reasonable	ma"uul ma"uule (f)
red	'aHmar Hamra (f) Humur (pl)
register at a hotel (vb)	nizil binzil
regular	"aadi "aadiyye (f) "aadiyyiin (pl)
religion	diin adyaan
rent (vb)	'ajar byaajur
repair (vb)	SallaH biSalliH
repairing	tasliiH
reservation	Hajz
reserve(vb)	Hajaz biHjiz
rest (vb)	staraaH bistriiH
rest	raaHa
restaurant	mat"am mataa"im
restroom	beet 'ilmayy
return (from) (vb)	riji" birja" (min)

returning	raaji" raaj"a (f) raaj"iin (pl)
rice	ruzz
rich	Gani Ganiyye (f) 'aGniya (pl)
ride (vb)	rikib birkab
riding	raakib raakbe (f) raakbiin (pl)
right (side)	yamiin
right, to your	"ala yamiinak
ring	xaatim
road	Tarii' Turu'
roasted	mHammar mHammara (f)
room	'uuDa 'uwaD; Gurfe Guraf
rooster	diik dyuuk

S

sack	kiis 'akyaas
safety	salaame
safety pin	dabbuus 'ingliizi
salad	SalaTa SalaTaat
salt	miliH
same	nafs
sanctuary	Haram
sanitary napkins	fuwaT siHiyye
sand	ramil
Saturday	ssabt
Saudi Arabia	ssu"uudiyye
say (vb)	'aal bi'uul
school	madrase madaaris
scissors	m'aSS m'aSSaat

second	taani taanye
see (vb)	šaaf bišuuf
seeing	šaayif šaayfe (f) šaayfiin (pl)
self	nafs
send (vb)	ba"at bib"at
September	'ayluul
service	xidme
seven	sab"a/sabi"/sab"
seventeen	sab"a ta"š/saba" ta"šar
seventh	saabii" saab"a
seventy	sab"iin
several	"iddit
~ times	"iddit marraat
shaving cream	ma"juun Hilaa'a
she	hiyye
ship	baaxira bawaaxir
shirt	'amiiS 'umSaan
shoes	jazme
shoes (dress ~)	kundara kanaadir
shoemaker	jazmaati
shop	dukkaan dakaakiin
shore	saaHil
short	'aSiir 'aSiira (f) 'iSaar (pl)
shower	duuš
shrimp	'reedis (coll)
sick	mariiD mariiDa (f) marDa (pl)
silk	Hariir
silver	fiDDa
simple	baSiiT baSiiTa (f) baSiiTiin (pl)

Sir	yaa siidi
sister	'uxt (f) xawaat
sit down (vb)	'a"ad bu'"ud
six	sitte/sitt
sixteen	sitt ta"š/sitt ta"šar
sixth	saadis saadse
sixty	sittiin
skirt	tannuura tananiir
sky	sama
sleep (vb)	naam binaam
sleeping	naayim nayme (f) naaymiin (pl)
slight	'aliil 'aliile (f) 'aliiliin (pl)
slippers	šibšib
slow	baTii'
slowly	šwayy, šwayy
small (young)	SGiir SGiire (f) SGaar (pl)
small	'aliil 'aliile (f) 'aliiliin (pl)
smoke (vb)	daxxan bidaxxin
soap	Saabuun
soccer	kurat lqadam
socks	kalsaat (pl)
some	ba"d; kam
someone	Had(a)
something	šii 'ašya(a')
sometimes	'aHyaanan; marraat
son	'ibin wlaad
soon	"an 'ariib
sorry	mit'assif mit'assfe (f) mit'assfiin (pl)
sort	noo" 'anwaa "
soup	šooraba

sour	HaamiD HaamDa
south	januub
southeast	januub šar'
southwest	januub Garb
speak (vb)	Haka biHki
spices	bhaaraat
spicy	Haarr
spinach	sabaanix (coll)
spoon	ma"la'a ma"aali'
sport	riyaaDa
spring	rabii"
standing	waa'if waa'fe (f) waa'fiin (pl)
star	najme njuum
start (vb)	bada bibda
state	dawle duwal; wilaaye wilaayaat
station	mHaTTa mHaTTaat
stay (vb)	bi'i bib'a
staying	naazil nazle (f) naazliin (pl)
step down (vb)	nizil binzil
stomach	mi"de
stomach ache	waja" baTin; waja" mi"de
stone	Hajr
stop (vb)	wa"f biwa"if
stopping	waa'if waa'fe (f) waa'fiin (pl)
stopping place	maw'if mawaa'if
store	maHall maHallaat
straight ahead	duGri
strange	Gariib

strawberries	freez (coll)
street	šaari" šawaari"
student	Taalib Taalibe (f) Tullaab (pl)
stuffed	maHši maHšiyye (f)
stuffed vegetable	maHši maHaaši
suburb	DaaHiy DawaaHi
sugar	sukkar
suit	badle badlaat
summer	seef
sun	šams
Sunday	l'aHad
suppose (vb)	Zann biZunn
surgery	"amaliyye
sweater	kinza
sweet	Hilu Hilwe (f) Hilwiin (pl)
sweets	Hilawiyaat
swim (vb)	sabaH bisbaH
swimming	sbaaHa
~ **pool**	birkit sbaaHa
~ **suit**	badlit sbaaHa
synagogue	ma"bad lyahuud
Syria	suuriyya
Syrian	šaami šaamiyye (f) šwaam (pl)
syringe	miHqana

T

table	Taawle Taawlaat
take (vb)	'axad byaaxud
take care!	diir baalak

tangerines	'afandi, yuusif 'afandi (coll)
tasty	Tayyib Tayybe (f)
tax	Dariibe Daraa'ib
taxi	taksi
tea	šaay
teacher	m"allim m"allime (f) m"allmiin (pl)
television	tilivizyoon
temple	ma"bad
ten	"ašra/"ašar/"ašr
tent	xeeme xeemaat
tenth	"aašir "aašre
than	min/min-/minn-/mni-
thank (vb)	šakar buškur
thank you	šukran
that	'illi
that, that he	'inno
theater	masraH
then	'izan
there is, there are	fii
they	humme
thing	šii 'ašya(a')
think (vb)	ftakar biftkir; Zann biZunn
third	taalit taalte
third (one third)	tult tlaat
thirteen	tlat ta"š/tlat ta"šar
thirty	tlaatiin
thousand	'alf 'aalaaf/taalaaf or 'uluuf
thread	xeeD

three	tlaate/tlaat/tlat
Thursday	lxamiis
ticket	tazkare tazaakir
round-trip ~	tazkare raayiH jayy
one-way ~	tazkare raayiH bass
ticket office	šubbaak ttazaakir
time	wa't
the same ~	nafs lwa't
tipping, tip	baGsiiš
tired	ta"baan ta"baane (f)
	taa"baaniin (pl)
to	"ala/"alee/"alay/"a-
today	lyoom
together	sawa
toilet paper	wara' tuwaaleet
tomatoes	bandoora (coll)
tomorrow	bukra
tonight	lleele
too	kamaan
tooth	sinn snaan
toothache	waja" snaan
toothbrush	furšit 'asnaan
toothpaste	ma"juun 'asnaan
total	majmuu" majmuu"aat
tour	jawla jawlaat
tourism	siyaaHa
tourist	saayiH saayHiin
towel	fuuTa fuwaT
town	balad (f) blaad
traditional	taqliidi
traffic	Harkit seer

train	qiTaar
translation	tarjame tarjamaat
travel (vb)	saafar bisaafir
travel	safar
travel agency	wakaalit siyaaHiyye
traveler	msaafir msaafriin (pl)
tree	šajar
trip	riHle riHlaat; safra safraat
truth, the	lHa'ii'a
Tuesday	ttlaata
turkey	diik Habaš
turnips	lift (coll)
TV show	musalsal musalsalaat
twenty	"išriin
two	tneen tinteen (f)

U

umbrella	šamsiyye
under	taHt
understand (vb)	fihim bifham
underwear	kalsoonaat
United States, the	lwilaayaat lmuttáHide
university	jaam(i)"a jaam(i)"aat
until	Hatta
upset stomach	talabbuk mi"de
usually	"aadatan

V

vaccination	talqiiH
valley	waadi widyaan

veal	laHmit "ijiil
vegetables	xuDra
very	jiddan
village	'arye qura
vine leaves	wara' "inab
vineyard	karm kruum
visit (vb)	zaar bizuur
visiting	zaayir zaayre (f)
	zaayriin (pl)

W

wait (vb)	stanna bistanna
walk (vb)	maša bimši
walking	maaši maašye (f)
	maašyiin (pl)
wall	suur
the Wailing ~	Haa'it lmabkaa
wallet	juzdaan
want (vb)	bid-/bidd-
warm	daafi
wash (vb)	Gasal biGsul
watch	saa"a saa"aat
water	mayy (f)
watermelons	baTTiix (coll)
way	Tarii'Turu'
we	niHna
wear (vb)	libis bilbas
wedding	"urs
Wednesday	l'arba"a
week	'usbuu" 'asabii"

welcome	marHaba; 'ahlan wa sahlan
well	mabSuuT mabSuuTa (f) mabSuuTiin (pl)
west	Garb
what (adj.)	'ayy
what (pron.)	'eeš; šuu
when	'eemta
where	feen; ween
which (adj.)	'ayy
while	w-/wi-
white	'abyaD beeDa (f) biiD (pl)
who; whom; whose	miin
why	leeš
wife	mara niswaan; zooje zoojaat
wind	hawa
window	šubbaak šababiik
wine	nbiid; xamir
winter	šita (m)
with	ma"
~ whom	ma" miin
without	bala; biduun
woman	mara niswaan
wood	xašab
wool	Suuf
word	kilme kilmaat
work (vb)	štaGal bištGil
work	"amal
world	"aalam; dinya
wound	jurH jruuH
write (vb)	katab buktub

wrong	Galat (invariable adj.)
what's ~ with him	šuu maalo

Y

year	"aam 'a"waam; sane sniin
yellow	'aSfar Safra (f) Sufur (pl)
yes	na"am; 'aywa
yesterday	mbaariH
yogurt	laban
you (m)	'inte
you (f)	'inti
you (pl)	'intu
young	SGiir SGiire´ (f) SGaar (pl)

Z

zero	Sifir

EASTERN ARABIC PHRASEBOOK

1. NUMBERS

CARDINAL NUMBERS

0	**Sifir**
1	**waaHad** (m), **waHde** (f)
2	**tneen** (m), **tinteen** (f)
3	**tlaate**
4	**arba"a**
5	**xamse**
6	**sitte**
7	**sab"a**
8	**tamaanye**
"	**tis"a**
10	**"ašra**
11	**Hda"š**
12	**tna"š**
13	**tlat ta"š**
14	**'arba" ta"š**
15	**xams ta"š**
16	**sitt ta"š**
17	**saba" ta"š**
18	**taman ta"š**
1"	**tisi" ta"š**
20	**"išriin**

In compound numbers above 20—the millions, thousands, hundreds, tens and units—are joined by w-/wi- *and*, for example 32 waaHad wlaaatin (lit. one and thirty)

21	waaHad w"išriin
22	tneen w"išriin
23	tlaate w"išriin
24	'arba"a w"išriin
25	xamse w"išriin
26	sitte w"išriin
27	sab"a w"išriin
28	tamaanye w"išriin
29	tis"a w"išriin
30	tlaatiin
40	'arb"iin
50	xamsiin
60	sittiin
70	sab"iin
80	tamaniin
90	tis"iin
100	miyye
101	miyye wwaaHad
102	miyye witneen
115	miyye wxamis ta"š
160	miyye wsittiin
175	miyye wxamse wsab"iin
200	miteen
300	tlat miyye
400	'arba" miyye
500	xamis miyye
600	sitt miyye
700	sabi" miyye
800	taman miyye
900	tisi" miyye
1,000	'alf

2,000	'alfeen
3,000	tlaat taalaaf
12,000	tna"šar 'alf
30,000	tlatiin 'alf
55,000	xamse wxamsiin 'alf
100,000	miit 'alf
1,000,000	malyoon
2,000,000	malyooneen
3,000,0000	tlat malayiin
12,000,000	tna"šar malyoon

ORDINAL NUMBERS

	masc.	fem.
first	'awwal	'uula
second	taani	taanye
third	taalit	taalte
fourth	raabi"	raab"a
fifth	xaamis	xaamse
sixth	saadis	saadse
seventh	saabi"	saab"a
eighth	taamin	taamne
ninth	taasi"	taas"a
tenth	"aašir	"aašre

When these words follow the noun they modify, they behave as regular adjectives: ššaari" lxaamis *the fifth street*. However, the ordinal frequently precedes the noun. In this case, the ordinal is always masculine singular: 'awwal marra *the first time*.

2. ETIQUETTE

Hello!	**marHaba**
Hello (in reply)	**marHabteen**
Nice to meet you.	**tšarrafna**
Good morning!	**SabaaH i̇lxeer**
Good morning (in reply)	**SabaaH i̇lxeer** or **SabaaH i̇nnuur**

The transition vowel, indicated in the transcription by an italic *i* or *u*, is a weak vowel glide that serves to interrupt a sequence of consonants, both within words and across word boundaries.

Good evening!	**masa lxeer**
Good evening (in reply)	**masa lxeer** or **masa nnuur**
Good night!	**leele sa'ʻiide**
Good night (in reply)	**sa'ʻiide mbaarake**
Good bye! (said by person remaining)	**ma'ʻ ssalaame**
Good bye (in reply)	*to a male* **'alla ysallmak**
	to a female **'alla ysallmik**
	to a group **'alla ysallimkum**
Good bye! (said by person leaving)	*to a male* **xaaTrak**
	to a female **xaaTrik**
	to a group **xaaTirkum**
Welcome!	**'ahlan wasahlan** or **'ahla wasahla**
Welcome (in reply)	*to a male* **'ahla wasahla fiik**

	to a female **'ahla wasahla fiiki**
	to a group **'ahla wasahla fiikum**
How are you?	**kiif lHaal?** *or*
	to a male **kiif Haalak?**
	to a female **kiif Haalik?**
	to a group **kiif Haalkum?**
Well, praise God.	*male speaking* **mabSuuT, ilHamdilla**
	female speaking **mabSuuTa, ilHamdilla**
	group speaking **mabSuuTiin, ilHamdilla**
So-so.	**maaši lHaal**
Thank you	**šukran**
You're welcome.	**"afwan**
No, thanks.	**la', šukran**
Please	*to a male* **tfaDDal**
	to a female **tfaDDali**
	to a group **tfaDDalu**
I'm sorry.	*male speaking* **'ana mit'assif**
	female speaking **'ana mit'assfe**
	group speaking **niHna mit'assfiin**
Happy holidays!	*to a male* **kull sane w'inte saalim**
	to a female **kull sane w'inte saalime**
	to a group **kull sane w'intum saalimiin**

Happy holidays (in reply)	*to a male* **w'inte saalim**
	to a female **w'inte saalime**
	to a group **w'intum saalimiin**
Congratulations!	**mabruuk**

3. INTRODUCTIONS

What's your name?	*to a male* **šuu 'ismak?**
	to a female **šuu 'ismik?**
My name is . . .	**'ismi . . .**

NATIONALITY

Where are you from?	*to a male* **'inte min feen?**
	to a female **'inti min feen?**
	to a group **'intu min feen?**
I'm from . . .	**'ana min . . .**
We're from . . .	**niHna min . . .**
America	**'ameerka**
England	**'ingiltra**
France	**fraansa**
Germany	**'almaanya**
Italy	**'iiTaalya**
Russia	**ruusya**
Spain	**sbanya**

AGE

How old are you?	*to a male* **'adeeš "umrak?**
	to a female **'adeeš "umrik?**
I'm . . . years old.	**"umri . . . sana**

FAMILY

Are you married?	*to a male* **'inte mijjawwiz?**

Eastern Arabic Dictionary & Phrasebook • 103

	to a female 'inti mijjawwze?
I'm (not) married.	*male speaking* 'ana (miš) mijjawwiz
	female speaking 'ana (miš) mijjawwze
Do you have children?	*to a male* "indak wlaad?
	to a female "indik wlaad?
I haven't any children.	maa fii "indi wlaad.
How many children do you have?	*to a male* kam walad "indak?
	to a female kam walad "indik?
I have . . .	"indi . . .
one girl	bint waHde
two girls	binteen
three girls	tlat banaat
one boy	Sabi waaHad
two boys	Sabiyeen
three boys	tlat Subyaan
family	"eele *or* 'ahil
father	'ab *or* waalid
my father	'abuuy
my stepfather	jooz 'immi
mother	'imm *or* waalde
my mother	'immi
my stepmother	mart 'abuuy
brother	'ax
my brother	'axuuy
sister	'uxt
my sister	'uxti

son	'ibn
my son	'ibni
daughter	bint
my daughter	binti
husband	zooj *or* jooz
my husband	zooji *or* joozi
wife	zooje *or* mara
my wife	zoojti *or* marti
grandfather	jidd
grandmother	sitt
uncle (father's brother)	"amm
uncle (mother's brother)	xaal
aunt (father's sister)	"amme
aunt (mother's sister)	xaale
cousin (m, from father's side)	'ibn "amm/e
cousin (m, from mother's side)	'ibn xaal/e
cousin (f, from father's side)	bint "amm/e
cousin (f, from mother's side)	bint xaal/e
friend (m)	SaaHib *or* Sadii'
friend (f)	SaaHibe *or* Sadii'e

LANGUAGE

Do you speak . . .	bitiHki . . .
Arabic?	"arabi?
English?	'ingliizi?
French?	fransaawi?
German?	'almaani?

Eastern Arabic Dictionary & Phrasebook • 105

Hebrew?	**"ibri?**
Italian?	**Tilyaani?**
Russian?	**ruusi?**
Spanish?	**sbanyooli?**

I speak a little bit ...	**baHki šwayy ...**
I don't speak ...	**maa baHki ...**
Did you understand?	*to a male* **fhimt?**
	to a female **fhimti?**
	to a group **fhimtu?**
Yes, I understood.	**na"am, fhimt**
Yes, we understood.	**na"am, fhimna**
No, I didn't understand.	**la', maa fhimt**
I didn't understand you.	**maa fhimt "aleek**
I didn't understand him.	**maa fhimt "allee(h)**

4. DIRECTIONS

Where is the post office?	**feen** *or* **ween 'ilbooSTa?**
Go straight ahead.	*to a male/female* **'imši duGri**
	to a group **'imšu duGri**
Please direct me to the Hotel Plaza.	*to a male* **min faDlak, dillni "ala 'uteel plaza**
Please direct me to the market.	*to a female* **min faDlik, dilliini "assuu'**
Please direct me to the post office.	*to a group* **min faDilkum, dilluuni "albooSTa**
Where is the restroom?	**feen beet 'ilmayy?**
Here.	**hoon**
Over there.	**hunaak**
To your right	*to a male* **"ala yamiinak**
	to a female **"ala yamiinik**
	to a group **"ala yamiinkum**
To your left	*to a male* **"ala šmaalak**
	to a female **"ala šmaalik**
	to a group **"ala šmaalkum**
Sorry, I don't know.	*male speaking* **mit'assif, maa ba"raf**
	female speaking **mit'assfe, maa ba"raf**
Where's a good restaurant?	**ween fii maT"am mniiH?**
Where is this bookstore?	**ween haadi lmaktabe?**
Between the post office and the hospital.	**been lbooSTa wilmustašfa**
Go to the office of tourism.	*to a male* **ruuHi "amaktab ssiyaaHa**

	to a female	**ruuHi "amaktab ssiyaaHa**
	to a group	**ruuHu "amaktab ssiyaaHa**
Please come along with me.	*to a male*	**tfaDDal ma"i**
	to a female	**tfaDDali ma"i**
Please come along with us.	*to a group*	**tfaDDalu ma""na**

5. TRAVEL

TAXI

Please send me a taxi.	**min faDlak 'ib"atli taksi**
I'd like to get a taxi to take me to . . .	**biddi taksi yaaxudni "ala . . .**
We'd like to get a taxi to take us to . . .	**bidna taksi yaaxudna "ala . . .**
Where do you want to go?	*to a male* **ween biddak truuH?**
	to a female **ween biddik truuHi?**
	to a group **ween bidkum truuHu?**
When do you want the taxi?	**'eemta biddak ttaksi?**
Please take me to . . .	**min faDlak xudni . . .**
the town	**"albalad**
the airport	**"almaTaar**
Please take us to the museum.	**min faDlak xudna "almatHaf**
How much will it cost?	**'adeeš l'ujra?**
Slow down.	**"ala mahlak**
I'm in a hurry.	*male speaking* **'ana mista"jil**
	female speaking **'ana mista"ijle**
We're in a hurry.	**niHna mista"ijliin**
I'll get off here.	**banzil hoon**
We'll get off in front of the hotel.	**ninzil 'uddaam l'uteel**
Stop here.	**wa"ifli hoon**
Please wait a moment.	**stanna šwayy**
Please wait here.	**stanna hoon**

Eastern Arabic Dictionary & Phrasebook • 109

BUYING TICKETS

Where is the ticket office?	**ween šubbaak ttazaakir?**
Where can I buy a ticket?	**ween mumkin aštri tazkara?**
I want to buy a ticket to . . .	**biddi aštri tazkare la . . .**
I want to buy a . . .	**biddi 'aštri . . .**
one-way ticket.	**tazkare raayiH bass**
round-trip ticket.	**tazkare raayiH jayy**
When do you want to go?	*to a male* **'eemta biddak tsaafir?**
	to a female **'eemta biddik tsaafri?**
	to a group **'eemta bidkum tsaafru?**
How much is the fare?	**'adeeš l'ujra?**
Are you a student?	*to a male* **'inte Taalib?**
	to a female **'inti Taalibe?**
	to a group **'intu Tullaab?**
No, I'm not a student.	**la', 'ana miš Taalib**
Do you want to travel first class or economy class?	**biddak tsaafir fi ddaraje l'uula willa fi ddaraje ttaanye?**
I want to travel economy class.	**biddi 'asaafir fi ddaraje ttaanye**
Do you smoke?	*to a male* **'inte bitdaxxin?**
	to a female **'inti bitdaxxni?**
	to a group **'intu bitdaxxnu?**
No, I don't smoke.	**la', 'ana maa badaxxin**

BUS

Where are you going?	**ween raayiH?**
I want to go to . . .	**biddi 'aruuH . . .**
Which bus goes to . . .?	**'ayy baas yaaxudni "ala . . .?**
This is the bus.	**Haada lbaaS**
Where is the nearest bus stop?	**ween 'a"rab maw'if lbaaS?**
When is the first bus to …?	**'eemta 'awwal baaS "ala . . .?**
When is the last bus to . . .?	**'eemta 'aaxir baaS "ala . . .?**
How long does the trip take?	**'adeeš btaaxud rriHle?**
The bus stops for half an hour.	**biwa"if 'lbaaS limuddat nuSS saa"a.**
I want to get off at the next stop.	**biddi anzil fi lmaw'if ttaali**
That's my bag.	**haada šantiti**
I have two bags.	**"indi šantiteen**

TRAIN

Which platform does the train leave?	**biyitla" ttreen min raSiif numra kam?**
I want to go from . . . to . . .	**biddi 'atla" min . . . w'anzil fi . . .**
Does the train stop at …?	**biwa"if ttreen fi . . .?**

AIRPLANE

What time does the airplane leave?	**'eemta bititla" TTayyaara?**
At what time do I have to be at the airport?	**'eemta laazim 'akuun fi lmaTaar?**

CAR

I would like to rent a car.	**biddi 'aajur sayyaara.**
Where is the nearest gas station?	**ween 'a'rab maHattit benziin?**
Where is the main road?	**ween *i*TTarii' rra'iisi?**
The car needs repairing.	**ssayyaara bidha tasliiH**
I want to get a good map of the Middle East.	**biddi 'alaa'i xaarTa mniiHa laššar' l'awSaT**
north	**šimmaal**
south	**januub**
east	**šar'**
west	**Garb**

TRAVELER'S CONVERSATION

How long have you been here?	*to a male* **'adeeš Sarlak hoon?**
	to a female **'adeeš Sarlik hoon?**
	to a group **'adeeš Sarlkum hoon?**
I have been here two days.	**Sarli hoon yoomeen.**
We have been here two weeks.	**Sarlna hoon 'usbuu"een.**
Where are you staying?	*to a male* **ween naazil?**
	to a female **ween naazle?**
	to a group **ween naazliin?**
I'm staying at the Hotel Plaza.	*male speaking* **'ana naazil fii 'uteel plaza**
	female speaking **'ana naazle fii 'uteel plaza**
	group speaking **niHna naazliin fii 'uteel plaza**

How did you come?	*to a male* **kiif 'ijiit?**
	to a female **kiif 'ijiiti?**
	to a group **kiif 'ijiitu?**
I came by plane.	**'ijiit fiTTayyaara.**
We came by car.	**'ijiina fissayyaara.**
How was your trip?	*to a male* **kiif kaan safirtak?**
	to a female **kiif kaan safirtik?**
	to a group **kiif kann safritkum?**
It was good, praise God.	**mniiHa, lHamdu lillaah.**

6. ACCOMMODATIONS AND HOTELS

I'm looking for a hotel.	**badawwir "ala 'uteel**
Where is . . .	**feen . . .**
a good hotel?	**'uteel mniiH?**
a clean hotel?	**'uteel nZiif?**
a cheap hotel?	**'uteel rxiiS?**
a nearby hotel?	**'uteel 'ariib min hoon?**
What is the address?	**šuu l"unwaan?**
Could you write it down, please?	**iktibli l"unwaan, min faDlak**

AT THE HOTEL

Do you have any rooms tonight?	**fii "indak 'uuDa faaDye lleele?**
Sorry, we're full.	**mit'assif, ma fii ayy 'uuDa faaDye**
I have a reservation.	**"indi Hajz**
My name is . . .	**'ismi . . .**
I want a room with a twin bed.	**biddi 'uuDa ma" taxt mifrid**
double bed.	**biddi 'uuDa ma" taxt mijwiz**
I want a room for two.	**biddi 'uuDa lašaxSeen**
I want a room . . .	**biddi 'uuDa . . .**
with a bathroom.	**ma" Hammaam**
ith a shower.	**ma" duuš**
with air conditioning.	**ma" takyiif**
with a balcony.	**ma" balkoona**
with a phone.	**ma" tilifoon**
with a TV.	**ma" tilivizyoon**
How much is the room?	**'adeeš si"ir l'uuDa?**

Can I see it?	**mumkin 'ašuufha?**
This hotel is very expensive.	**haada l'uteel Gaali ktiir**
How long will you be staying?	*to a male* **'adeeš raHtib'a hoon?**
	to a female **'adeeš raHtib'i hoon?**
	to a group **'adeeš raHtib'u hoon?**
I'm staying here for	**raH'ab'a hoon . . .**
one day.	**yoom waaHid bass**
two days.	**yoomeen**
one week.	**limuddat 'usbuu"**
two weeks.	**limuddat 'usbuu"een**
Do you have any ID?	**"indak hawiyye?**
I'd like to speak to the manager.	**baHibb 'aHki ma" lmudiir, min faDlak**

NEEDS

I need . . .	**baHtaaj . . .**
toilet paper	**wara' tuwaaleet**
soap	**Saabuun**
another towel	**fuuTa taanye**
an extra blanket	**Hraam taani**
Please clean the room.	**min faDlik naZZfi l'uuDa**
Please give me the key.	**min faDlak, 'a"tiini limuftaah**
I have lost my key.	**xasirt limuftaaH**
The water has been cut off.	**'inqaTa"at lmayy**
The electricity has been cut off.	**'inqata"at lkahrabe**

ACCOMMODATIONS

The air conditioning
doesn't work.
'ittakyiif xarbaan

The toilet is blocked.
'ittuwaaleet masduud

I cannot open the
window.
**ma ba'dar 'aftaH
ššubaak**

Wake me at seven
o'clock in the morning.
**fayyi'ni ssaa"a sab"a
SSubuH**

I would like to pay
the bill.
biddi 'adfa" liHsaab

May I pay with
my ... card?
**mumkin 'adafa" bikart
Master, Visa, etc.?**

7. FINANCE

Where is the bank?	**ween lbank?**
I want to change some money.	**biddi 'aSruf maSaari**
Where can I change some money?	**ween mumkin 'aSruf maSaari?**
I want to cash this check.	**biddi 'aSruf haada ššek**
What is the exchange rate?	**'addeeš si'ir ttaHwiil?**
What is the commission?	**'addeeš "umuulit ttaHwiil?**
I want to change $200.	**biddi 'aSruf miteen duulaar**
I don't have any change.	**ma "indi fakka**
Do you have change for a pound?	**mumkin tfkili jneeh?**
US dollars	**duulaar 'ameerkaani**
British pounds	**jneeh sterliini**
traveler's checks	**šekaat siyaaHiyye**

8. FOOD AND DRINK

EATING OUT

The important thing is to find a clean place and good food.	**lmuhimm nlaa'i maHall naZiif, w'akil Tayyib**
The Salaam Restaurant isn't bad.	**maT"am ssalaam miš baTTaal**
It's inexpensive.	**huwwe rxiiS**
Is there any other?	**fii Geero?**
There is an Italian restaurant next to the hotel.	**fii maT"am Tilyaani jamb l'uteel**
Let's go to the National Restaurant.	**xalliina nruuH "almaT"am lwaTani**
What will you order?	*to a male* **šuu btu'mur?**
	to a female **šuu btu'mri ?**
	to a group **šuu btu'umru?**
What do you have?	**šuu fii "indkum?**
What do you want to eat?	*to a male* **šuu bitriid ta'kul?**
	to a female **šuu bitriidi ta'kli?**
	to a group **šuu bitriidu ta'klu?**
Please bring me . . .	**min faDlak, jibli . . .**
Please bring us . . .	**min faDlak, jibilna . . .**
Do you want anything sweet?	*to a male* **bitriid šii Hilu?**
	to a female **bitriidi šii Hilu?**
Please give me the bill.	**min faDlak, 'a"tiini liHsaab**

Please give us the bill.	**min faDlak, 'a"tiina liHsaab**

breakfast	**fTuur**
lunch	**Gada**
dinner	**"aša**

SETTING THE TABLE

bottle	**'anniine**
bread	**xubz**
butter	**zibde**
cup	**finjaan**
fork	**šooke**
glass	**kaas**
knife	**sikkiin**
menu	**liista**
napkin	**fuuTa**
pepper	**filfil**
plate	**SaHin**
salt	**miliH**
spoon	**ma"la'a**

MEAT AND FISH

meat	**laHme**
beef	**laHmit ba'ar**
chicken	**jaaj**
fish	**samak**
ham	**jambon**
lamb	**laHmit xaruuf**
liver	**kibde**
pork	**laHmit xanziir**

FOOD AND DRINK

shrimp	**'reedis**
turkey	**diik Habaš**
veal	**lahim "ijiil**
boiled	**masluu'**
broiled	**mašwi**
fried	**ma'li**
roasted	**mHammar**
stuffed	**maHši**
a bowl of soup	**SaHin šooraba**
two bowls of soup	**SaHneen šooraba**
a salad	**SaHin SalaTa**
spices	**bhaaraat**

FRUITS

almonds	**looz**
apples	**tuffaaH**
apricots	**mišmiš**
bananas	**mooz**
cherries	**karaz**
dates	**tamir**
figs	**tiin**
lemons	**leemuun** *or* **haamiD**
melon	**šimmaam**
mulberries	**tuut**
oranges	**burd'aan**
peaches	**durraa'**
pears	**njaaS**
plums	**xoox**
strawberries	**freez**

| tangerines | yuusif 'afandi *or* 'afandi |
| watermelon | baaTTix |

VEGETABLES

vegetables	xuDra
artichokes	'arDi šooki
(dry broad) beans	fuul
(French) beans	luubya
(haricot) beans	faSuulya
beets	šamandar
cabbage	malfuuf
carrots	jazar
cauliflower	'arnabiiT
chickpeas	Hummus
cucumbers	xyaar
eggplants	beetinjaan
garlic	tuum
lentils	"ads
lettuce	xaSS
mint	na"na"
okra	baamye
olives	zeetuun
onions	basal
parsley	ba'duunis
peas	bisilla
potatoes	baTaaTis
radishes	fijil
spinach	sabaanix
tomatoes	bandoora
turnips	lift

FOOD AND DRINK

HAVING A DRINK

Would you like anything to drink?	*to a male* **btu'mur tišrab šii?**
	to a female **btu'mri tišrabi šii?**
Let's drink a cup of coffee.	**xalliina nišrab finjaan 'ahwe**

In ordering things, Arabic uses the independent form of the number followed by a singular noun:

One coffee.	**waaHad 'ahwe**
Two coffees	**tneen 'ahwe**
How would you like the coffee?	*to a male* **kiif bitHibb l'ahwe**
	to a female **kiif bitHibbi l'ahwe?**
	to a group **kiif bitHibbu l'ahwe?**
With sugar or black?	**Hilwe willa saada?**
One with sugar and one black.	**waaHad Hilwe, waaHad saada**
Do you have beer?	**fii "indkum biira?**
I'm sorry, We don't have beer.	**mit'assif, maa fii "inna biira**
Bring me one tea.	**jibli waaHad šayy**
How would you like the tea?	*to a male* **kiif btHibb ššayy?**
Weak or strong?	**xafiif willa ti'iil?**
Weak, please.	**xafiif, min faDlak**
But don't make it too sweet.	**bass balaaš ykuun Hilu ktiir**
Please bring us some water.	**min faDlak, jibilna mayy**

122 • *Eastern Arabic Dictionary & Phrasebook*

beer	**biira**
coffee	**'ahwe**
hot chocolate	**kakaw**
ice	**talj**
juice	**"aSiir**
milk	**Haliib**
tea	**šayy**
water	**mayy**
wine	**nbiid**

BUYING FOOD

Do you have any fruit?	**maa fii "indkum fawaakih?**
Of course we have.	**ma"luum, "inna**
Give me a little watermelon.	**'a"tiini baTTiixa Sgiire**
Bring me some grapes, please.	**jibli "inab, min faDlak**
Give me three watermelons.	**'a"tiini tlat baTTiixaat**
We need a few vegetables.	**laazimna šwayyit xuDra**
What do you have that's fresh?	**šuu fii "indak šii Taaza?**
Everything I have is fresh.	**kullši "indi Taaza**
Give me just one fish.	**'a"tiini bass samake**
How many oranges do you give me for a pound?	**kam burd'aan bta"tiini bliira?**
Put out two kilos for me.	**Huttilli tneen kilo**
Do you want something else?	**btu'mur šii taani?**

9. SHOPPING AND SERVICES

Do you know where there is a . . .	biti"rafli ween fi . . . hoon?
bakery	maxbaz
bank	bank
barber	Hallaa'
bookstore	maktabe
clothing store	maHall mlaabis
grocery	ba'aale
hairdresser	kuwafeer
gift shop	maHall yibii" 'a"maal yadawiyye
market	suu'
newsstand	dukkaan jaraa'id
pharmacy	Saidaliyye
shoemaker	jazmaati
travel agency	wakaalit siyaaHiyye

What can I do for you?	'ayy xidme?
I want to buy ...	biddi 'aštri . . .
I'm just looking.	bašuuf bass
Do you have . . . ?	"indak . . .
How much do you want?	'addeeš biddak?
Can you write down the price?	mumkin tiktibli ssi"ir?
That's two much.	haada ktiir
I don't have much money.	maa "indi maSaari ktiir
Two pounds is enough.	bikaffi liirteen
I give you a pound and a half.	ba"tiik liira wnuSS
Please send this to the hotel.	min faDlak b"atli haada "al'uteel

COLORS

black	**'aswad**
blue	**'azra'**
brown	**binni**
green	**'axDar**
gray	**ramaadi**
red	**'aHmar**
white	**'abyaD**
yellow	**'aSfar**

CLOTHES AND ACCESSORIES

bag	**šanta**
belt	**Hzaam**
blouse	**bluuze**
dress	**fuSTaan**
dress shoes	**kundara**
a pair of shoes	**'aHdiyye**
hat	**burneeta**
necktie	**gravaat**
pants	**banTaloon**
shirt	**'amiiS**
skirt	**tannuura**
socks	**kalsaat**
sweater	**kinza**
umbrella	**šamsiyye**
underwear	**kalsoon**

KINDS OF CLOTH

What kind of cloth do you want?	**šuu noo" li'maaš lli biddak yyaa?**
cotton	**'uTun**

linen	**kittaan**
silk	**Hariir**
wool	**Suuf**

GIFTS

box	**Sanduu'**
bracelet	**suwaar**
brass	**nuHaas 'aSfar**
carpet	**sijaade**
copper	**nuHaas**
earrings	**Hala'**
embroidery	**taTriiz**
enamel	**miina'**
gold	**dahab**
handicraft	**'a"maal yadawiyye**
iron	**Hadiid**
jewelry	**mjawharaat**
leather	**jild**
metal	**ma"din**
necklace	**"iqd**
pottery	**faxxaar**
ring	**xaatim**
silver	**fiDDa**
stone	**Hajr**
traditional	**taqliidi**
wood	**xašab**

TOILETRIES

adhesive bandage	**"iSaaba**
comb	**mišT**
deodorant	**muziil rraa'iHa**

hairbrush	**furšit ša'ir**
razor	**muusa**
safety pin	**dabuus 'ingliizi**
sanitary napkins	**fuwaT siHiyye**
shampoo	**šampuu**
shaving cream	**ma"juun Hilaa'a**
soap	**Saabuun**
tissue	**mandiil**
toilet paper	**wara' tuwaaleet**
toothbrush	**furšit 'asnaan**
toothpaste	**ma"juun 'asnaan**

STATIONARY

book	**ktaab**
dictionary	**qaamuus**
envelope	**Zarf**
magazine	**majalle**
map	**xaarTa**
newspaper	**jariide**
writing paper	**wara' kitaaba**
pen, pencil	**'alam**
postcard	**kart booSTaal**
scissors	**m'aSS**

Do you have any foreign publications?	**fii "indak 'ayy jaraa'id min lxaarij?**

PHOTOGRAPHY

How much is it to develop this film?	**'addeeš taHmiiD lfilm?**
When will it be ready?	**'eemta raHykuun jaahiz?**

B&W (film)	**film 'abyaD w'aswad**
color film	**film mulawwan**
camera	**kaameera**

SMOKING

cigarettes	**sagaayir**
cigars	**sigaaraat**
filter-tipped cigarette	**sigaarit filtar**
lighter	**'addaaHa**
matches	**kibriit**
pipe	**biiba**
tobacco	**duxaan**

ELECTRICAL APPLIANCES

adapter	**wuSla muhaaya'a**
battery	**battaariyye**
fan	**marwaHa**
iron	**Hadiid**
plug	**sidaade**
radio	**raadyo**
television	**tilivizyoon**

AT THE LAUNDRY

I have five shirts to be washed and ironed.	**fii "indi xamis 'umSaan, Gasiil wkawi**
We have three pairs of pants to be cleaned and pressed.	**fii "indna tlat banTaloonaat, tanZiif wkawi**
When do you want them?	**'eemta biddak yyaahum?**
The day after tomorrow, if possible.	**ba"d bukra, 'iza mumkin**

AT THE BARBER'S

How do you want me to cut your hair?	**kiif biddak 'a'usillak ša"irak?**
Please shorten it a bit on top.	**xaffifli yyaa šwayy min foo'**
Please comb it dry.	**min faDlak, maššTo "annaašif**
Do you want a shave?	**biddak tiHli' da'nak?**
No, thanks.	**la', mamnuun**

10. SIGHTSEEING AND ENTERTAINMENT

It there a guide who speaks English?	**fii daliil biHki 'ingliizi?**
What is that?	**šuu haada?**
Where is the entrance?	**ween lmadxal?**
May I take a photograph?	**masmuuH ttaSwiir?**
What time does it open?	**'eemta biftaH?**
What times does it close?	**'eemta bisakkir?**
How much is the entrance fee?	**'adeeš l'ujra?**
What's there to do in the evening?	**šu mumkin ni"mal filmasa?**
Where can I hear local folk music?	**ween mumkin 'astama" 'ila musiiqa arabiyye?**
When is the wedding?	**feen l"urs?**
What time does it begin?	**'eemta bibtada"?**

beach	**šaTT lbaHar**
cemetery	**ma'bare**
center	**markaz**
church	**kniise**
dancing	**ra's**
exhibition	**ma"rad**
(arabic) folk music	**musiiqa "arabiyye**
market	**suu'**
monastery	**deer**
monument	**'atar**
mountain	**jabal**
mosque	**jaami"**
museum	**matHaf**
old city	**lmadiine l'adiime**
palace	**'aSir**

park	**muntazah**
party	**Hafle**
school	**madrase**
synagogue	**ma"bad lyahuud**
temple	**ma"bad**
theater	**masraH**
tower	**borj**
university	**jaam(i)"a**
wall	**suur**

11. COMMUNICATIONS

AT THE POST OFFICE

Where is the post office?	**feen'ilbooSTa?**
What time does the post office open?	**'eemta btiftaH lbooSTa?**
What time does the post office close?	**'eemta bitsakkir lbooSTa?**
I would like to send a letter to the U.S.	**biddi 'ab"at maktuub "ala ameerka**
Would you like to send it by regular mail or by airmail?	**biddak tib"ato bilbariid l"aadi willa bilbariid ljawwi?**
How long will it take to get to the U.S. by airmail?	**'adeeš byaaxud lmaktuub Hatta yasal ameerka bilbariid ljawwi?**
How many stamps do I need to mail this?	**'addeeš baHtaaj Tawaabi"?**
Please give me five regular stamps and ten airmail stamps.	**min faDlak, 'a"tiini xamis Tawaabi" "aadiyye w"ašar Tawaabi" bariid jawwi**
I have an airmail letter that I want to send registered to America.	**fii ma"i maktuub Tayyaara biddi 'ab"ato msajjal la'ameerka**

airmail	**bariid jawwi**
envelope	**Zarf**
letter	**maktuub**
postcard	**kart booSTaal**
registered mail	**bariid msajjal**
stamp	**Taabi"**

TELEPHONING

Where is the nearest public phone?	**ween 'a'rab tilifoon?**
I would like to make a phone call.	**biddi 'a"mal mukaalame tilifooniyye**
Can I telephone from here?	**mumkin 'a"mal mukaalame tilifooniyye min hoon?**
Hello? Who's speaking?	**haloo? miin "ambiHki?**
This is . . .	**'ana . . .**
Is this the Hotel Plaza?	**hoon 'uteel plaza?**
Yes, who do you want?	*to a male* **na"am, miin bitriid?**
	to a female **na"am, miin bitriidi?**
I'd like to speak to . . .	**baHibb 'aHki ma" . . .**
One minute, please.	*to a male* **d'ii'a, min faDlak**
Is . . . there?	*asking for a male* **. . . mawjuud?**
	asking for a female **. . . mawjuude?**
He's not here now.	**huwwe miš mawjuud halla**
She's not here now.	**hiyye miš mawjuude halla**
When will he be back?	**'eemta birja"?**
When will she be back?	**'eemta btirja"?**
He'll be back at three.	**birja" ssaa"a tlaate**
Would you like to leave a message?	*to a male* **bitriid titriklo xabar?**
I'm sorry, wrong number.	*male speaking* **mit'assif, numra galat**

female speaking
mit'assfe, numra Galat

SENDING A FAX

I would like to send a fax.　**biddi 'ab"at faks**

Where can I send a fax?　**ween mumkin 'ab"at faks?**

How much do you charge per page?　**'adeeš bitkallif safHa?**

12. EMERGENCY

Could you help me please?	*to a male* **mumkin tsaa"idni, min faDlak?**
	to a female **mumkin tsaa"idiini, min faDlik?**
Call the police!	**'uTlub ššurta!**
I'll call the police!	**'ana aTlub ššurTa!**
Where is the police station?	**ween maxfar ššurTa?**
Go away!	**imši!**
Get out of here!	**barra!**
There's been a car accident.	**Hasal Haadis sayyaara**
Thief!	**Haraami!**
My ... has been stolen.	**sara'u . . . li**
I have lost ...	**xasirt . . .**
my handbag.	**ššantiti**
my money.	**MaSaari li**
my passport.	**jawaaz safar li**
my credit card.	**cart . . . li**
I have a problem.	**"indi muškile**
I want to contact the US consulate.	**biddi 'ataSSil bil'unSliyye l'ameerkaaniyye**
I want to contact the US embassy.	**biddi 'ataSSil bissafaara l'ameerkaaniyye**
I need an interpreter.	**baHtaaj mtarjim**

13. HEALTH CARE

Where it the nearest doctor?	**ween a'rab duktoor?**
Where is the nearest hospital?	**ween a'arab mustašfa?**
I need to call an ambulance.	**laazim banaadi sayyarit l'is''aaf**
Where is the nearest pharmacy?	**ween a'rab saydaliyye?**

CHECK-UP

What's the trouble?	*to a male* **šuu maalak?**
	to a female **šuu maalik?**
I am sick.	*male speaking* **'ana mariiD**
	female speaking **'ana mariiDa**
How did it start?	**kiif saarat lmuškile?**
When did it start?	**'eemta saarat lmuškile?**
How long have you been in bed?	*to a male* **'adeeš Sarlak filfarše?**
	to a female **'adeeš Sarlik filfarše?**
It's been two days.	**Sarli yoomeen**
I have been vomiting.	**kunt 'astafriG**
I can't eat.	**ma ba'dar 'aakul**
I can't sleep.	**ma ba'dar anaam**
Are you better today?	**nšalla 'aHsan lyoom?**
I'm a little better.	**lHamdilla, 'aHsan šwayy**
The fever went away today.	**lyoom, raaHat lHaraara**

I want to see another doctor.	**biddi 'ašuuf duktoor taani**
I have . . .	**"indi . . .**
a cough.	**su"aal**
a headache	**waja" raas**
a slight cold	**šwayyit rašiH**
an allergy	**Hassaasiyye**
constipation	**'imsaak**
cramps	**tašannujaat**
diarrhea	**'ishaal**
fever	**Hamaawa** or **sxuuune**
influenza	**'influwenza**
stomach ache	**waja" mi"de** or **waja" baTin**
tooth ache	**waja" snaan**
an upset stomach	**talabbuk mi"de**
I'm pregnant.	**'ana Haamil**
I'm allergic to . . .	**"indi Hassaasiyye didd . . .**

MEDICATION

I take this medication.	**baaxud haada ddawa**
I need medication for . . .	**baHtaaj dawa li . . .**
When do I have to take it?	**'eemta laazim aaxud ddawa?**
You have to take two pills daily.	*to a male* **laazim taaxud Habteen kull yoom**
	to a female **laazim taaxdi Habteen kull yoom**
One after lunch and one after dinner.	**waHde ba"d lGada wwaHde ba"d l"aša**
One before breakfast.	**waHde 'abil lfTuur**

It is possible for me to travel?	**mumkin asaafir?**
What should I do?	**šu laazim 'a"mal?**

HEALTH WORDS

antibiotic	**'antibiyotik**
blood	**dam**
blood group	**zumra damawiyye**
blood pressure	**daGt damawi**
blood transfusion	**na'l ddam**
cancer	**saraTaan**
contagious	**saari**
dentist	**duktoor l'asnaan**
diabetes	**maraD lbawl ssukari**
fever	**Hamaawa** *or* **sxuuune**
flu	**bard**
germs	**jaraatiim**
heart attack	**nawbe 'albiyye**
infection	**"adwaa**
needle	**'ibre**
nurse	**mumarriDa**
pill	**Habbe**
snake bite	**"addit Hayye**
surgery	**"amaliyye**
syringe	**miHqana**
thermometer	**miizaan lHaraara**
vaccination	**talqiiH**

THE BODY

bone	**"azm**
eye	**"een**

nose	**'anf**
mouth	**tumm**
breast	**Sidr**
belly	**baTin**
hand	**'iid**
finger	**'iSba"**
knee	**rukbe**
leg	**rijil**
foot	**'adam**
head	**raas**
ear	**daan**
neck	**raqaba**
shoulder	**kitf**
back	**Zahir**
elbow	**koo"**
skin	**jild**

EYESIGHT

I have broken my glasses.	**kassart naZZaaraati**
Can you repair them?	**mumkin tsalliha?**
How much are you going to charge for it?	**'addeeš raHtaaxud "aleeha?**
When will they be ready?	**'eemta raHtkuun jahze?**
contact lenses	**"adasaat laaSi'a**
contact lense solution	**munaZZif lil"adasa**

14. TIME AND DATES

What time is it?	**'adeeš ssaa"a?**
It's one o'clock.	**ssaa"a waHde**
It's two o'clock.	**ssaa"a tinteen**
It's three o'clock.	**ssaa"a tlaate**
It's five minutes past six.	**ssaa"a sitte wxamse**
It's six fifteen.	**ssaa"a sitte wrubu"**
It's six twenty.	**ssaa"a sitte wtult**
It's six twenty-five.	**ssaa"a sitte wnuSS ('i)lla xamse**
It's six thirty.	**ssaa"a sitte wnuSS**
It's six thirty-five.	**ssaa"a sitte wnuSS wxamse**
It's a quarter to six.	**ssaa"a sitte ('i)lla rubu"**
It's twenty to six.	**ssaa"a sitte ('i)lla tult**
Come after one minute.	*to a male* **ta"aal ba"d d'ii'a**
Come on time.	*to a female* **ta"aali "alwa't**
Come after five minutes.	*to a group* **ta"aalu ba"d xamis da'aa'yi**

DAYS OF THE WEEK

Sunday	**(yoom) l'aHad**
Monday	**(yoom) ttineen**
Tuesday	**(yoom) ttlalaata**
Wednesday	**(yoom) l'arba"**
Thursday	**(yoom) lxamiis**
Friday	**(yoom) ljum"a**
Saturday	**(yoom) ssabt**

MONTHS OF THE YEAR

January	**kaanuun (t)taani**
February	**šbaat**
March	**'aadaar**
April	**niisaan**
May	**'ayyaar**
June	**Hzeeraan**
July	**tammuuz**
August	**'aab**
September	**'ayluul**
October	**tišriin (l)'awwal**
November	**tišriin (t)taani**
December	**kaanuun (l)'awwal**

FEAST DAYS AND HOLIDAYS

Birthday	**"iid miilaad**
Christmas	**"iid lmiilaad**
Easter	**"iid lfisiH**
Independance Day	**"iid listiqlaal**
New Year's Eve	**"iid raas ssane**
Birthday of the Prophet	**"iid lmawlid**
Breaking the Fast of Ramadan	**"iid lfiTir**
Feast of the Sacrifice	**"iid l'aDHa**

15. WEATHER

How's the weather?	**maa Haalit Ta'S?**
What's the temperature?	**maa darajit lHaraara?**
It's very warm today.	**šoob ktiir lyoom**
It's very cold today.	**bard ktiir lyoom**
The weather is nice.	**'iTTa'S mumtaaz**
Please open the window.	*to a male* **min faDlak, iftaH ššubbaak**
Please close the door.	*to a female* **min faDlik sakkri lbaab**
rain	**maTar**
wind	**Hawa**

THE SEASONS

spring	**rrabii"**
summer	**SSeef**
fall	**lxariif**
winter	**ššita**

ARABIC LANGUAGE TITLES
FROM HIPPOCRENE

Dictionaries

Arabic-English/English-Arabic Concise Dictionary, *Romanized*
Egyptian and Syrian Dialect
4,500 entries • 325 pages • 4 x 6 • 0-7818-0686-0 • W • $12.95pb • (775)

Arabic-English/English-Arabic Standard Dictionary
30,000 entries • 455 pages • 5½ x 8½ • 0-7818-0383-7 • W • 24.95pb • (195)

Arabic-English/English-Arabic Dictionary and Phrasebook
Useful to those traveling throughout the Middle East and Africa, this book presents a standard Arabic and provides both the Arabic script and its romanized transliteration.
250 pages • 3¾ x 7 ½ • 0-7818-0973-8 • W • $11.95 • (445)

Arabic for Children

Hippocrene Children's Illustrated Arabic Dictionary
English-Arabic/Arabic-English
Hippocrene offers a delightful antidote to the assumption that difficult languages cannot be taught in a playful way with this illustrated children's dictionary. Featuring 500 Arabic words in their original spelling along with easy-to-use English pronunciation, this dictionary provides an invaluable basis for learning Arabic at an early age.
500 entries • 94 pages • 8½ x 11 • 0-7818-0891-X • W • $11.95pb • (212)

Arabic Language Guides

Mastering Arabic
Book and Audio Cassettes
320 pages • 5¼ x 8¼ • 0-87052-922-6 • USA •
$14.95pb • (501)
2 cassettes: 0-87052-984-6 • USA • $12.95 • (507)

Emergency Arabic Phrasebook
This book gives aid workers, students, travelers and
foreign dignitaries the essential words and phrases at
their fingertips when they need them most.
80 pages • 7½ x 4½ • 0-7818-0976-2 • NA • $5.95 • (467)

Saudi Arabic Basic Course
Reflecting a preference for "modern" words and
structure, this guide gives the student working profi-
ciency in the language to satisfy social demands and
business requirements.
288 pages • 6½ x 8½ • 0-7818-0257-1 • W •
$14.95pb • (171)

Arabic for Beginner's
Revised Edition
204 pages • 5½ x 8½ • 0-7818-0841-3 •
$11.95 • (229)

Prices subject to change without prior notice. To order
Hippocrene Books, contact your local bookstore, call (718)
454-2366, visit www.hippocrenebooks.com, or write to:
Hippocrene Books, 171 Madison Avenue, New York, NY
10016. Please enclose check or money order adding $5.00
shipping (UPS) for the first book and $.50 for each addi-
tional title.